The Jews of Iberia

A SHORT HISTORY

Juan Marcos Bejarano Gutierrez

Yaron Publishing

Juan Marcos Bejarano Gutierrez/Yaron Publishing
701 Forest Park Place
Grand Prairie, Tx 75052
www.cryptojewisheducation.com

Book Layout ©2017 BookDesignTemplates.com

Ordering Information:
Quantity sales. Special discounts are available on quantity purchases by corporations, associations, and others. For details, contact the "Special Sales Department" at the address above.

The Jews of Iberia/ Juan Marcos Bejarano Gutierrez. —1st ed.
ISBN 978-1537118147

Contents

The Jews of the Iberian Peninsula 7

The Islamic Conquest of Spain 14

    The Almoravides (1040–1147) 18

    The Almohades (1121–1269) 19

The Christian Reconquest of Spain 23

Jewish Life in Christian Spain..25

    The Massacres of 1366...27

The Riots of 1391 31

    The Public Trial of Ferrant Martinez 32

    Ferrant Martinez Appointment as Vicar-General 33

    The Attack on the Community of Majorca 38

The Aftermath 42

Conversos among Jews and Christians....................................46

    Vicente Ferrer and the Jewish Community 51

    The Tortosa Disputation 55

A Shared Destiny..64

    The Establishment of the Inquisition 65

The Forced Conversions in Portugal 74

Conclusions..82

To Conversos of the Past who were lost to the Jewish Community and to those struggling to return.

The rise of the Conversos can only be understood in the context of the broader Jewish experience in Spain. I recently published the title *Secret Jews: The Complex Identity of Crypto-Jews and Crypto-Judaism*. This work was based on my final doctoral project at the Spertus Institute of Jewish Studies. It discusses both the history of Jews forced to convert to Christianity in Spain and Portugal as well as many of the social and theological challenges they confronted in Jewish and Christian communities.

I realize, however, that many people simply do not have the time to read a more comprehensive study on Conversos or on Sephardic history in general. My goal has been to write short works that allow the reader to learn about a topic without feeling overwhelmed. This book will hopefully provide the interested reader with a more digestible review of both Sephardic and Converso history. This book includes an overview of Jewish life in the Iberian Peninsula from its early days through the Expulsion. It does not address the theological or *halakhic* issues that many Conversos faced when they returned to Jewish communities. I hope, however, that the information included will spur the reader to continue their study of this fascinating subject.

Juan Marcos Bejarano Gutierrez

.

CHAPTER 1

The Jews of the Iberian Peninsula

The history of Jews in Spain and Portugal spans more than a thousand years. By most measures, it is even longer than the large-scale settlement of Jews in the land of Israel which was interrupted several times in Jewish history. Legends ascribe the arrival of the earliest settlers to the days of the biblical prophet Obadiah, but archeologically speaking, the first record of Jews is much later.

An early testament to the presence of Jews in the Iberian Peninsula is a decree issued by the Council of Elvira in southern Spain circa 304 CE. The Christian Council was comprised of bishops and presbyters from the cities of Córdoba, Seville, Toledo, Saragossa, and various other towns populated by Jews. The council prohibited Christians from living or eating with Jews. It also barred Christians from allowing their daughters to marry Jews or pagans. Christians were also forbidden from asking Jews to bless their fields. The penalty for failing to comply with these rules was excommunication.

The Visigoths gained control over most of the Iberian Peninsula in the waning years of the Western Roman Empire. The Visigoths were initially pagans. They converted to Arian Christianity and eventually to Orthodox Christianity. After 586 CE, Visigoth rule was characterized by anti-Jewish legislation.[1] In 551 CE, Athangild, one of many aspirants vying for the Visigoth throne requested support from the Eastern Roman Empire (Byzantine). The Byzantines supported his claim and also seized Córdoba, Granada, Cartagena, and the Balearic Islands in the process.[2] Furthermore, Byzantine anti-Judaism influenced the entire Visigoth kingdom. Byzantine rule in southern Spain ended in 625 CE, but its influence over the Visigoths persisted.

The Conversion of Reccared to Catholicism by Antonio Muñoz Degrain

[1] José Hinojosa Montalvo, "Los judíos en la España medieval: de la tolerancia a la expulsión." Lecture, Universidad de Alicante, 1998,
http://rua.ua.es/dspace/bitstream/10045/13209/1/Hinojosa_Jud ios_España.pdf.
[2] Norman Roth, *Jews, Visigoths, and Muslims in Medieval Spain: Cooperation and Conflict* (Leiden: E.J. Brill, 1994), 7.

At the third ecclesiastical Council of Toledo in 589, King Reccared prohibited Jews from acquiring or owning Christian slaves. They were also barred from public office and banned from having intercourse with Christian women. The circumcision of either a slave or a Christian was punished with confiscation of property. The council also stipulated that children born of the intermarriage between a Jew and a Christian were to be baptized and reared as Christians. However, King Reccared was only partially successful in enforcing these laws. King Reccared resisted the attempts by Jews to rescind these decrees and earned praise from Pope Gregory I (540-604 CE) for his steadfastness.[3]

Successive church councils in Toledo were focused on preventing Jewish converts to Christianity from reverting to Judaism. Many of these Jews appear to have converted under duress and the weight of increasing anti-Jewish measures. Jewish converts were prohibited from associating with openly practicing Jews. The children of those suspected to have relapsed were seized and transferred to Christian families. Recent converts were also bound to sign a formal declaration that they had abandoned Jewish rituals and observances.[4]

In 613, King Sisebut demanded that all Jews residing in his domains convert. He commanded that all Jews

[3] Solomon Grazyel, "The Beginnings of Exclusion," The Jewish Quarterly Review, New Series, Vol. 61, No.1 (1970): 23.

[4] Cecil Roth, *A History of the Marranos* (Philadelphia : Jewish Publication Society, 1947), 9.

were to either submit to baptism or leave within a year. According to Catholic sources, ninety thousand Jews converted to Christianity.[5] The Islamic chronicler, Al-Razi, contends that all Iberian Jews converted to Christianity though later Church councils confirmed the continued existence of non-converted Jews in Spain.[6]

The forced conversions were severely criticized by the leading Spanish theologian of the day, St. Isidore of Seville. Despite his condemnation, during the fourth Toledo Council convened in 633, St. Isidore insisted that forced converts live a Christian life lest the Christian faith be considered worthless.[7] The fourth Toledo Council noted the ongoing Jewish practices of forced converts who were treated as blasphemers.[8] They lost their children and slaves if the latter had been circumcised.[9] Previously adopted laws, including forbidding contact between Jewish converts and unconverted Jews, were reiterated. Also, a convert to

---

[5] Ibid., 7.

[6] "And other Jews outside of the land of Spain came to settle [the places] which these [Jews of Spain] had left." Norman Roth, *Jews, Visigoths, and Muslims in Medieval Spain: Cooperation and Conflict* (Leiden: E.J. Brill, 1994), 13.

[7] Canon 57.

[8] Norman Roth, *Jews, Visigoths, and Muslims in Medieval Spain: Cooperation and Conflict* (Leiden: E.J. Brill, 1994), 31.

[9] The topic of *relapsi,* baptized Jews who reverted to Jewish practices, was discussed repeatedly in 506, 633, 638, 654, 655, 681, and 693 CE. Henriette-Rika Benveniste, "On the Language of Conversion: Visigothic Spain Revisited," Historein 6 (2006): 74, 79.

Christianity, whose sincerity was dubious, was excluded from giving testimony in a court of law.[10]

Following the death of King Sisebut in 621 CE, King Swinthila (circa 621-631) assumed the throne. According to Al-Razi, Jews from other territories settled in Spain during his reign. Swinthila was forced to relinquish his throne and was succeeded by Sisenand. King Sisenand ruled briefly from 631–636 CE.[11] Under Sisenand's reign, children of converted Jews were taken from their parents' custody and given to Christians or to monasteries to ensure they received a proper Christian education. Forced converts, known to practice Jewish ceremonies, were given away as slaves.[12] King Sisenand was succeeded by King Chintila, who reigned from 636–640 CE.

At the sixth Toledo council in 638 CE, Jews were forced to make a declaration known as the *Placitum*. The statement described all the Jewish observances, the Sabbath, holidays, and other practices from which they pledged to desist. [13] Moreover, Jewish converts vowed to

---

[10] Solomon Grazyel, "The Beginnings of Exclusion," The Jewish Quarterly Review, New Series, Vol. 61, No.1 (1970): 23–24.

[11] Bat- Sheva Albert, "Isidore of Seville: His Attitude towards Judaism and His Impact on Early Medieval Canon Law," The Jewish Quarterly Review, LXX, Nos 3-4 (1990): 216-217.

[12] Interestingly, St. Braulio, the Bishop of Saragossa, wrote to Pope Honorius I inquiring why baptized Jews were allowed to return to Judaism when they arrived in Rome. Bat- Sheva Albert, "Isidore of Seville: His Attitude towards Judaism and His Impact on Early Medieval Canon Law," The Jewish Quarterly Review, LXX, Nos 3-4 (1990): 214.

avoid contact with unbaptized Jews and not marry them.[14] King Receswinth (649-672 CE) outlawed all Jewish observances, including circumcision, the laws of *kashrut*, Jewish weddings, and banned Jews from appearing in court.

In 654 CE, another "declaration of faith" was presented by Jewish converts of Toledo to King Receswinth. The document made reference to the fact that Jewish practices had been observed by Jews who had nominally converted to Christianity decades before under the reign of King Chintila or possibly as far back as under King Sisebut. [15]

Under the direction of King Erwig (circa 680-687), the twelfth Toledo Council decreed that any unconverted Jews still living throughout Visigoth territory were to convert. If they refused, their property was to be confiscated, and they would be expelled. King Erwig enacted harsh punishments for observing circumcision and reading anti-Christian writings. Egica, the son-in-law of King Erwig, succeeded him as king. King Egica confiscated all assets owned by Jews and declared all Jews, baptized or not, to be slaves offered to Christians as gifts. Jewish children over the age of seven were taken from their parents and also given away as slaves. The last

---

[13] Norman Roth, *Jews, Visigoths, and Muslims in Medieval Spain: Cooperation and Conflict* (Leiden: E.J. Brill, 1994), 23.

[14] Ibid.

[15] Paul Halsall, Jewish History Sourcebook: The Jews of Spain and the Vis-igothic Code, 654-681 CE. Retrieved 22 November 2012 from Ford-ham University:
http://www.fordham.edu/halsall/jewish/jews-visigothic1.asp

Council of Toledo was convened in 694 CE. It decreed that the property of Jews was to be confiscated and that they were to be exiled from their homes and sold into slavery to prevent them from observing Judaism.[16]

---

[16] Solomon Grazyel, "The Beginnings of Exclusion," The Jewish Quarterly Review, New Series, Vol. 61, No.1 (1970): 25.

CHAPTER 2

The Islamic Conquest of Spain

The Islamic invasion of Spain in 711 radically changed the position of Jews throughout the Iberian Peninsula. The conquest was rapid, and the cities of Córdoba, Malaga, Granada, Seville, and Toledo were placed in charge of their Jewish residents as the Muslim armies moved northwards. The change in conditions was highly significant. Restrictions, which had previously affected the Jewish community, were finally lifted. Furthermore, some Jews served as advisors and guides to the advancing Muslim forces. Within the confines of Islamic law, Jews, as well as Christians, were religiously tolerated. As *dhimmis,* they were required to pay a tribute of one golden dinar per person and follow various restrictions for non-Muslims.

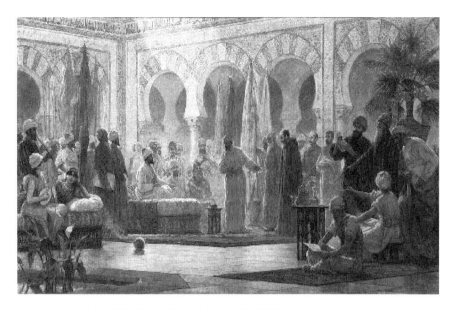

The Caliphate of Cordoba under Abd-al-Rahman III
by Dionisio Baixeras Verdaguer

Under the rule of the Ommiad ruler, Abd al-Raḥman I (circa 731-788 CE), a prosperous kingdom was established with the city of Córdoba as its capital. During his reign, many Jews served the caliphate in critical positions. Jews enjoyed both stability and prosperity under the reigns of Abd al-Raḥman I and his son Al-Ḥakim. Under Islamic rule, Spain emerged as a refuge for the Jews oppressed in other parts of the world. The cities of Córdoba and Lucena in Spain flourished as centers of Jewish learning while the caliphate ruled most of the Peninsula from 756–1031.

The unique conditions created under Islamic rule which lasted until the early 12th century CE is termed as *Convivencia.*[17] For some, the term connotes a near utopian society in which Jews, Christians, and Muslims lived and worked side by side in almost idyllic symbiosis.[18] There is no doubt that Iberian Jewry experienced a period of relative stability and success during this time, at least when compared to Jews living in Christian societies in Central or Eastern Europe. Under Islamic rule, Jews were not the dominant or sole minority community. In Christian lands, Jews—except for the occasional Christian heretical group —were the primary focus of attention for those looking to establish a homogenous religious and cultural society. Under Islam, Jews, various types of Christians, as well as Zoroastrians, and members of other religious faiths shared the spotlight as religious minorities.

But the extent of that success, beyond the ranks of the great Jewish poets, philosophers, and courtiers of roughly a two hundred years plus period, is likely overstated.[19] While there were positive interactions between the three communities, this does not suggest an unbroken state of

---

[17] Ibid., xii.

[18] Norman Roth, *Conversos, Inquisition, and the Expulsion of the Jews from Spain* (Madison: University of Wisconsin, 1995), 9. There is something to be said for the unique circumstances of Jews within Spanish society. The Fuero de Cuenca relates: "If a Jew and a Christian contest something, they designate two neighboring townspeople, one Christian and one Jewish." Also, in the Fuero de Sepulveda, a Jew's testimony, was considered as a valid as a Christian's. Joseph Perez, *History of a Tragedy: The Expulsion of the Jews from Spain* (Chicago: University of Illinois Press, 1993), 123.

[19] Joaquim Carvalho ed., *Religion and Power in Europe: Conflict and Convergence* (Pisa: Edizioni Plus - Pisa University Press, 2007), 78.

harmony between them. Distrust, prejudice, and conflict were also part of the equation. [20]

From the 11th to the 13th century, some incidents of violence by Muslims towards Spanish and Moroccan Jews occurred. These include the Muslim massacre of the Jews of Fez in 1035 and an attack on the Jews of Granada in 1066. Moreover, around the year 1105, the Jews of Lucena were forcibly converted to Islam. Muslim authorities suppressed a Jewish revolt in Córdoba in 1117. The revolt was spurred by the belief that the Messiah was soon to be revealed. In 1127, Islamic authorities repressed another Jewish messianic revolt in Fez. Jews were forcibly converted in Spain between 1146 and 1163. Forced conversions of Jews in Morocco also occurred from 1164 to 1185. Violent atrocities continued to be committed against Jews as a new Muslim massacre took place in Marrakesh in 1232 followed by another in Fez in 1275.[21]

In those cases where Islamic persecution did break out, it was typically levied against all members of the *dhimmi* class. The violence erupted in a significant part because of violations by members of the class that was thought to impact the superior status of Muslims. Nevertheless, the clashes were largely different from the

---

[20] Joseph Perez, *History of a Tragedy: The Expulsion of the Jews from Spain* (Chicago: University of Illinois Press, 1993), xii. Elie Kedourie, *Spain and the Jews: The Sephardi Experience 1492 and After* (London: Thames and Hudson, 1992), 33.

[21] Allan Harris Cutler and Helen Elmquist Cutler, *The Jews as Ally of the Muslim: Medieval Roots of Anti-Semitism* (Notre Dame: University of Notre Dame, 1986), 259.

type of violence and discrimination faced by Jews in Christian lands. As Bernard Lewis notes, in Islamic society, antagonism against Jews was non-theological.[22]

The Almoravides (1040–1147)

The conquests of King Alfonso VI of Castile caused Al-Mu'tamid, the last independent king of Andalusia, to summon help from King Yusuf ibn Tashfin of the growing Almoravid Empire in North Africa. The religious sect that ibn Tashfin commanded was known as the Almoravides. The battle of Zallaka resulted in an Almoravid victory and staved off further Christian conquest for the time being.[23] As a consequence, Yusuf ibn Tashfin gained supreme power on the Islamic side. The Almoravides were religious zealots, and with their support, ibn Tashfin attempted to force the Jewish community of Lucena to convert to Islam.

During the rule of his son Ali (1106–43 CE), Islamic attitudes towards Jews were more positive. Some Jews were appointed collectors of royal taxes while others were allowed to serve in governmental positions, including those of "vizier" or "nasi." The communities

---

[22] Bernard Lewis, *The Jews of Islam* (Princeton: Princeton University Press, 1984), 85.

[23] The degree of Jewish integration in both Christian and Muslim camps is highlighted in part by the battle of Zallaka in October 1086. King Alfonso's army purportedly included 40,000 Jews. The battle purportedly was not initiated until after the Sabbath had ended. In addition to inquiring from his bishops, Alfonso also asked Jewish scholars and astrologers about their predictions for the battle.

of Seville, Granada, and Córdoba which had suffered previously were rebuilt.

The Almohades (1121–1269)

The religious zealotry of the Almoravides was surpassed by Abdallah ibn Tumart in Morocco in 1112. Ibn Tumart established the new Islamic party known as the Almohades or the Muzmotas. He saw himself as a purist defender of Mohammed's original teachings relating to the unity of G-d. Following the death of Abdallah, Abd al-Mu'min assumed leadership and strove to eliminate the Almoravides as both political and religious rivals.

Abd al-Mu'min invaded southern Spain and overthrew the Almoravides. Córdoba was captured in 1148 while Seville, Lucena, Montilla, and other cities were taken within a year. The Almohades, as they had done in Africa, forced Jews to either convert to Islam or face death.[24] Abraham ibn Daud, the renowned Spanish

---

[24] An Egyptian Jew writing in the year 1148 relates that when Abd al-Mu'min, the successor of Ibn Tumart, subjugated Oran, he slaughtered the Almoravid garrison, killed the governor, and gibbeted his corpse. In Fez, he allegedly slaughtered 100,000 persons and another 150,000 in Marrakesh. He also executed the whole population of Tilimsen, with the exception of those Jews who converted to Islam. After subjugating Sijilmasa, a city that did not repel his attack, the Almohades attempted to force the Jewish residents to convert to Islam. Nothing came of the discussions for seven months. When the new governor took office, he gave the Jewish population an ultimatum: either conversion or death. Approximately, 150 Jews were put to death for their refusal to convert. The rest, led by a local rabbinic judge, accepted the "genial invitation" to adopt Islam. From the city Bejaia (Bougie)

Jewish chronicler, characterized the years of the Almohad conquest as "years of calamity, evil decrees, and religious persecutions [shemad] [which] befell Israel." He also noted that there were some Jews who "were marked for leaving the faith at the threat of the sword…" Ibn Daud ascribed the following words to Ibn Tumart: "Come let us cut them off from being a nation so that the name of Israel may be no more in remembrance…he left them neither name nor remnant in his entire kingdom."[25]

The persecutions under the Almohades lasted for ten years. Regarding the harshness of the attacks, Maimonides stated,

> "You know, my brethren that on account of our sins G-d has cast us into the midst of this people, the nation of Ishmael, who persecute us severely, and who devise ways to harm us and to debase us. This is as the Exalted had warned us; 'Even our enemies themselves being judges' (Deuteronomy 32:31). No nation has ever done more harm to Israel. None has matched it in debasing, humiliating, and hating us."[26]

---

on the eastern Algerian coast to Gibraltar, no one professing "the name Jew…remains; he who was killed was killed, he who sinned [by converting to Islam] sinned." Herbert Davidson, *Moses Maimonides: The Man and His Works* (Oxford: Oxford University Press, 2005), 10.

[25] Ibid., 11.

[26] Moses Ben Maimon, The Epistle to Yemen, Trans. Norman A. Stillman, *The Jews of Arab Lands: A History and Source Book* (Philadelphia: Jewish Publication Society, 1979), 241.

The Battle of Las Navas de Tolosa
by Francisco de Paula Van Halen

In 1160, the Muslim historian Ibn al-Athir stated that when the Almohades conquered "Ifriquiya," which likely refers to the area around Tunis, they compelled Jews and Christians to choose between Islam and death.[27] Some Jews apparently resisted the onslaught of the Almohades even though they proved unsuccessful.[28] Many Jews

---

[27] Herbert Davidson, *Moses Maimonides: The Man and His Works* (Oxford: Oxford University Press, 2005), 15.

[28] Joseph Ibn Aqnin, a Moroccan Jewish writer in the 12th century, also provided a description of the actions taken under the Almohade regime. Ibn Aqnin relates that Jewish inheritances were

converted to Islam in a superficial manner, while others fled to Castile, where King Alfonso VII received them openly, particularly in Toledo. Almohad power lasted until the Battle of Navas de Tolosa on July 16, 1212, when they were defeated. Islamic authority in the Iberian Peninsula declined rapidly. In a few years, they were driven back to the Kingdom of Granada, which remained largely intact until the end of the 15th century.

---

confiscated; Jews were barred from engaging in trade, the Jewish ownership of slaves was banned, Jews were required to dress differently as to be easily identified, and their children were taken from them to be raised as Muslims. Ibn Aqnin notes that many of the descendants of those who did convert to Islam returned to Judaism in the second and third generations. Ibid., 13.

CHAPTER 3

The Christian Reconquest of Spain

The steady Christian conquest of the Peninsula saw the relocation of Jews to Christian territory. This process was guaranteed, in part, by the legislation of King Ferdinand I of Leon in the 11ᵗʰ century, which offered Jews a haven. As a consequence of military successes against the Muslim *taifas* (i.e. city states), which rose after the demise of the Omayyad Caliphate, Christian kings found large swathes of conquered territory under inhabited.

Many Muslims remained in these newly conquered territories. A Jewish presence helped resettle the land and offset potential concerns over Muslim fealty. Jewish linguistic and diplomatic skills served the Christian sovereigns well in the ongoing relationship, and at times, warfare with the Muslim Kingdom of Granada and the remaining independent city states.

From the 13ᵗʰ to the 15ᵗʰ centuries, the Hispanic kingdoms of the Iberian Peninsula were home to the largest Jewish communities of the European continent. Jose Hinojosa Montalvo estimates that near the end of the 13th century, 100,000 Jews lived in Castile alone. By the latter part of the 14th century, the population had grown between 180,000 to 250,000. The most inhabited Jewish quarters, consisting of 3,000 or more people, were found in the cities of Toledo, Barcelona, Zaragoza, Valencia, Majorca, Seville, Córdoba, Tudela, Granada, and Lucena.[29]

Unfortunately, growing tension brought about by economic hardship and diseases increased the anti-Jewish sentiment already fostered by Christianity. Jews were depicted as heretics and subversive, unleashing attacks on various Jewish quarters. The island of Majorca off the eastern coast of the Peninsula was attacked in 1309, and in 1328 the Jewish communities of the Kingdom of Navarre were nearly exterminated.[30] In 1349 in Catalonia, with the advent of the *Black Death*, the bubonic and pneumonic plague, Jews were blamed for the onset of the catastrophe.[31]

---

[29] José Hinojosa Montalvo, "Los judíos en la España medieval: de la tolerancia a la expulsión." lecture, Universidad de Alicante, 1998, http://rua.ua.es/dspace/bitstream/10045/13209/1/Hinojosa_Jud ios_España.pdf

[30] Cecil Roth, *A History of the Marranos* (Philadelphia: Jewish Publication Society, 1947), 11.

[31] Natalie Oeltjen, "Crisis and Regeneration: The Conversos of Majorca, 1391 – 1416" (PhD diss., University of Toronto, 2012), 12.

CHAPTER 4

Jewish Life in Christian Spain

King Pedro I of Castile, the son, and successor of King Alfonso XI ruled between 1350 and 1369. He was positively inclined toward the Jews in his domains. Under his reign, Jews reached the peak of their influence in Christian Spain. From the start of his reign, Pedro gathered so many Jewish courtiers that his detractors mocked his court as a "Jewish" court. Inner rivalry in the royal family led to a series of bloody civil wars that devastated Castile along with its Jewish communities. Both parties to the civil war mulled the question of Jewish influence on the royal court. The supporters of Henry Trastamara, the aspiring usurper to the throne and Pedro's half-brother, accused Pedro of having been the son of a Jew, who was then substituted for the legitimate royal son. Trastamara secured the support of the nobility who regarded King Pedro I as too pro-Jewish.

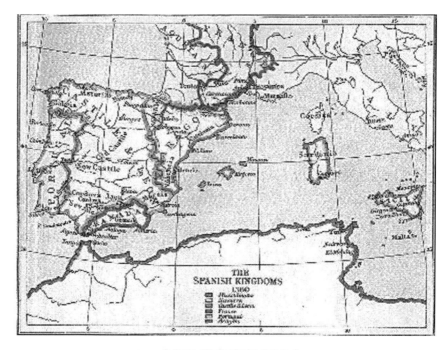

The Spanish Kingdoms in 1360
by Francisco de Paula Van Halen

On May 7th, 1355, Henry de Trastamara invaded a section of the Jewish quarter of Toledo. His forces attacked and murdered thousands of people. However, Henry de Trastamara and his followers were unable to take control of the central section of the Jewish quarter. Some Jews in that area had received reinforcements from certain Toledo noblemen and were able to defend themselves. Five years later in 1360, Henry marched again through Castile with the assistance of King Pedro IV of Aragon. When the former reached Najera, he ordered the massacre of the Jews there. Those living in Miranda de Ebro were also attacked.

While King Pedro continued the war effort, Henry enlisted the services of mercenaries led by Bertrand du Guesclin——a Breton cavalier and French army commander. The mercenaries under Guesclin attacked Jews wherever they found them. In Briviesca, near the city of Burgos, 200 Jewish families were reportedly murdered. Henry was proclaimed King in Calahorra and entered Burgos on March 31st, 1366. The new king levied a substantial tax on the Jews of Burgos. The Jews of Segovia and Avila also had their property seized. The Jews of Toledo had remained loyal to King Pedro and were also made to endure the burden of maintaining Henry's troops, and they were heavily fined. The deposed King Pedro requested aid from the Prince of Wales. Faced with these reinforcements, Henry was forced to escape, but his departure was short-lived as he returned to Castile with additional troops.

The Massacres of 1366

The Jewish populations of Villa Diego, Aguilar, and other towns were attacked and destroyed by Henry's forces. The communities of Paredes and Palencia met with a similar fate. The residents of Valladolid, who pledged homage to Henry, plundered the Jews of their city. They destroyed their houses and synagogues and even shredded their Torah scrolls. 300 Jewish families from Jaen were also detained as prisoners and taken to Granada.

Henry de Trastamara

According to the contemporary writer, Samuel Ẓarẓa of Palencia, the distress reached its peak in Toledo. Henry laid siege to the city, and thousands died through starvation.[32] The civil war ultimately ended when King Pedro was captured and beheaded by Henry and Bertrand Du Guesclin on March 14th, 1369. Henry de Trastamara ascended the throne as King Henry II.

[32] Singer, Isidore; Adler, Cyrus; (eds.) The Jewish Encyclopedia, "Spain." Last modified 1904. Accessed January 2, 2013. http://www.jewishencyclopedia.com/articles/13940-spain.

Once in power, King Henry II forged a policy towards Jews that mitigated the actions he had previously perpetrated against the Jewish community. The Jewish communities of Castile formed a historically significant group that filled some important roles for the crown and also provided extensive contributions to the royal exchequer. While amity with the king was the most active defense against violence, this very loyalty to the reigning monarch could be used against them by a usurper.

Regardless of his dislike for Jews, King Henry utilized their services. He employed wealthy Jews such as Samuel Abravanel and Joseph Pichon, among others, as financial councilors and tax-collectors. In 1371, the Cortes of Toro demanded that Jews be barred from royal palaces. They were not allowed to hold public office. Members of the Cortes argued that Jews should be forced to live apart from Christians, desist from wearing expensive clothes, not ride mules, wear distinctive badges, and cease from using Christian names. The King agreed to the last two demands. His agreement that Jews wear distinctive badges made him the first Castilian monarch to follow this directive previously established by Rome. He also agreed to a request made by the Cortes of Burgos in 1379 that Jews be prohibited from bearing or selling weapons. He did, however, allow Jews to retain the right to criminal jurisprudence. The trend towards limiting Jewish rights continued with the Cortes of Soria in 1380. The Cortes declared that rabbis and the heads of the Jewish quarters were forbidden under penalty of a fine, to impose the penalties of death, disfigurement, expulsion, or excommunication. However, Jews were allowed to select their judges in civil proceedings.[33]

In contrast to their kinsmen in the eastern part of the Peninsula, the Jews of Lisbon were left undisturbed by the violence that became characteristic of the Kingdom of Castile. The first significant violence against the Portuguese Jewish community erupted during the conflict between Dom Ferdinand of Portugal and Henry Trastamara II of Castile. In 1373, the Castilian army entered Lisbon. The invading army sacked the Jewish quarter in the area of Rua Nova, and several Jews were killed. Further harm against the Jews of Lisbon was brought about by the grand master of the Knights of St. Bennett of Aviz, who eventually succeeded Dom Ferdinand and was later crowned King John I.

---

[33] E.H. Lindo, *The Jews of Spain and Portugal* (London: Longman, Brown, Green, & Longmans, 1848), 153-155, 162.

CHAPTER 5

The Riots of 1391

The popular sentiment against the Jewish community, already stoked during the Castilian civil war, was increased by the malicious sermons of Ferrant Martinez of Seville. Martinez initially served the Archdeacon of Ecija and vociferously called for the destruction of the twenty-three synagogues in Seville and the confinement of Jews to their quarter to prevent unnecessary contact with Christians.[34] The leaders of the Jewish community repeatedly tried to curtail his endeavors. Martinez promised his listeners that the royal court would not discipline any attack initiated by them.[35] He used this power to compel the magistrates of Alcalá de Guadeyra and Ecija among other cities to no longer tolerate Jews in their vicinity.

---

[34] Yitzhak Baer, *A History of the Jews in Christian Spain: Volume 2* (Philadelphia: Jewish Publication Society, 1961), 95.

[35] Ibid., 96.

His activities were sufficiently troublesome to the Jewish community of Seville to appeal to King Henry II. The King ordered the Archdeacon not to intrude into the affairs of his subjects or incite the people against them. He was to abstain from deciding legal disputes between them. Jews in the area were granted permission to withdraw from the Archdeacon's jurisdiction. The Jewish community complained to King John I four years later regarding Martinez's continuing activities. King John I reproved Martinez on March 3rd, 1382 with little effect. This was followed up with a new edict on August 25th, 1383. This time, he castigated the Archdeacon and threatened severe punishment.

The Public Trial of Ferrant Martinez

On February 11th, 1388, Martinez, and Judah Aben Abraham, a representative of the Jewish community of Seville, appeared before the *alcaldes mayores* Ferrant Gonzalez and Ruy Perez along with their respective witnesses. Abraham referred to the two royal edicts previously issued and demanded that the Archdeacon should desist once and for all from any arbitrary and unlawful acts against the community. Failure to do so would result in the community's immediate appeal before the King.

Despite this threat, Martinez pledged to continue to preach as he had previously. He argued that everything he had done was on the advice of the Archbishop and was motivated by his longing for the welfare of the Church and the king alike. Martinez claimed the Jewish community had offered him a bribe for adjudicating a significant case in their favor. The episcopal chapter intervened and sent two of its members to the king. They made it clear that the Archdeacon was overriding the authority of the Pope and that the safety of the Jewish community was being compromised. Through the likely influence of his wife Leonora, the king ruled that while Jews were under his protection and should not be mistreated, the Archdeacon's zeal was praiseworthy and that matters should not be further exacerbated.

Ferrant Martinez Appointment as Vicar-General

The danger Ferrant Martinez posed was appreciated in 1388 by the Archbishop of Seville, Pedro Gomez Barroso. Barroso condemned Martinez as contemptuous and suspect of heresy. He convened a body of experts in canonical law and summoned Martinez to repudiate his previous actions. The latter was adamant and refused to recant. As a consequence, he was prohibited from performing any clerical functions or deciding any case, on penalty of excommunication.

To add to the conflict, King John I of Castile died suddenly in an accident. He was succeeded by his adolescent son, Henry III, who was guided in part by a young stepmother. Ferrant Martinez was the confessor to the Queen Mother, Leonora.[36] Under the reign of the eleven-year-old King Henry III, Martinez's fortunes changed drastically. On July 7th, 1390 the Archbishop

---

[36] Cecil Roth, *A History of the Marranos* (Philadelphia: Jewish Publication Society, 1947), 12.

died, giving Ferrant room to maneuver even more freely. Ferrant became the Administrator of the Diocese, which gave him power over the local ecclesiastical council. In a dramatic turn of events, the archiepiscopal chapter chose Martinez as Vicar General. On December 8th, 1390, Ferrant Martinez called upon the clergy of his diocese to destroy all synagogues in their parishes and send to him all lamps, Hebrew books, and Torah scrolls. Martinez argued the synagogues were havens of the Devil. The clergy of Ecija and Alcalá de Guadeyra obeyed, and the synagogues of Soria and Santillana were damaged. The Jewish community of Seville appealed to the king. A few days later, the court responded by sending a letter to the archiepiscopal chapter holding it accountable for all reparations due to the Jewish community. This included an order to rebuild and repair any synagogues that had been damaged or destroyed. The king also gave orders that Martinez be removed from his post. Ferrant Martinez countered by arguing that an ecclesiastical official was subject to the Church and not to the king. The king, he argued, had no right to depose him from office, or require that he restore the damaged and destroyed synagogues.[37]

In early January 1391, prominent Jews assembling in Madrid received information that riots were on the verge of breaking out in Seville and Córdoba. Juan Alfonso de Guzman, Count of Niebla and governor of the city, and his relative, the Sheriff Mayor Alvar Perez de Guzman, ordered the arrest and public beating of two of the

---

[37] Mark D. Meyerson, *A Jewish Renaissance in Fifteenth-Century Spain* (Princeton: Princeton University Press, 2004), 23.

rioters' leaders. Instead of lowering tensions, several Jews were murdered and robbed. The Guzman brothers were threatened with death.[38]

On June 6th, 1391, mobs attacked the Jewish quarter of Seville. The chronicler Pedro López de Ayala reported that 4,000 Jews were killed. According to Rabbi Hasdai ibn Crescas, even Christian nobles joined in to reap plunder. Thousands of Jews converted to avoid death. From Seville, the onslaught spread to the surrounding cities and villages, including Alcalá de Guadeyra, Cazalla, Fregenal, Carmona, Ecija, and Santa Olalla. Many wanted to unleash similar violence against the Muslims living in their midst. The fear that retaliation would be brought against Christians in the Kingdom of Granada ended this desire.[39]

King Joan (John) of Aragon instructed his brother, Prince Marti, on July 3rd, to take the necessary measures to protect Jews since "some unbridled and incorrigible persons" were speaking against them. Rabble-rousers from Castile had arrived in the capital and exacerbated the situation.[40] By July 9th, the violence reached Valencia on the eastern side of the Peninsula. The mob was led by approximately forty or fifty Christian youths. As they

---

[38] Rica Amran Cohen, "Judíos y conversos en las crónicas de los Reyes de Castilla (desde finales del siglo XIV hasta la expulsión)," Espacio, Tiempo y Forma. Serie III. Historia medieval 9 (1996): 259.

[39] Kenneth R. Scholberg, "Minorities in Medieval Castilian Literature," Hispania, Vol. 37, No. 2 (1954): 203.

[40] Mark D. Meyerson, *A Jewish Renaissance in Fifteenth-Century Spain* (Princeton: Princeton University Press, 2004) 23.

marched, they carried a blue banner with a white cross and several makeshift crosses made out of bamboo. They reached the Jewish quarter, "shouting that the Archdeacon of Castile is coming with his cross and that all the Jews should be baptized or die."[41]

When the day ended, the Christian mob now comprised of "vagabonds and foreigners and people of lesser and poor condition...men of the Order Montesa and ...mendicants...knights...and mean of peerage and squires" had slaughtered several hundred Jews. The majority of the Jews of Valencia were forcibly baptized by the Friar Vicente Ferrer. The Jewish community of Valencia, which had once numbered 2,500, now numbered only 200 who had managed to escape the violence and coerced conversions.[42]

By the 16th of July, the violence spread to Córdoba where the entire Jewish quarter was destroyed, and the violence continued through Montoro, Andujar, Jaen, Ubeda, and Baeza in the heart of Andalusia. At least 2,000 Jews were killed. By June 20th, the attacks reached Toledo. Among those who perished, were the descendants of the famous Toledo Rabbi Asher ben Yehiel.[43] Murcia alone was spared, but the entire community of Ciudad Real was either slaughtered or converted. The communities of Huete and Cuenca

---

[41] Yitzhak Baer, *A History of the Jews in Christian Spain Volume 2* (Philadelphia: Jewish Publication Society, 1961), 100.

[42] Mark D. Meyerson, *A Jewish Renaissance in Fifteenth-Century Spain* (Princeton: Princeton University Press, 2004), 22.

[43] Yitzhak Baer, *A History of the Jews in Christian Spain Volume 2* (Philadelphia: Jewish Publication Society, 1961), 98.

survived but were not left unscathed by the violence. In Madrid, the news of the massacres reached the ears of its inhabitants and most, if not all Jews, were baptized in a preemptive move to avert violence.

The only community, which was left untouched in the region of Valencia, was Morvedre.[44] Within a week of the attack on the Jewish quarter of Valencia, a large number of people journeyed to Morvedre and rioted there. The quick action of the local bailiff, Bonafonat de Sant Feliu was critical, and the Jewish community was saved. They escaped the violence by moving into the local fortified castle. The actions of Sant Feliu were reinforced by various knightly families in the area who ensured that the local Jewish population was protected.[45] The violence in Valencia was reported throughout the kingdom, and the Jews in Alzira, Xativa, Castello, Borriana, and Lliria converted.

On July 16th, news of the rioting reached the King of Castile and his regents in the city of Segovia in the region of Old Castile and León. The king and his councilors were limited in their ability to stem the violence other than stressing to their councils the importance of saving the Jewish communities that were the official properties of the Crown. The ineffectual power of the Crown was demonstrated by the fact that even Segovia was not entirely free of the violence. In the northern reaches of Castile, in the Cuenca del Duero, many Jews converted

---

[44] Ibid., 102.

[45] Mark D. Meyerson, *A Jewish Renaissance in Fifteenth-Century Spain* (Princeton: Princeton University Press, 2004), 24, 27.

while others fled the cities to escape the violence.[46] Seventy towns and cities in Castile had experienced violence.[47] The Kingdom of Portugal was spared the violence due to the diligent actions of its king.

The Attack on the Community of Majorca

By August 2nd, the violence reached Palma, in Majorca. The riots coincided with civil rest. The mobs, who attacked the Jewish communities of Majorca, Girona, and Barcelona, and all parts of the Kingdom of Aragon, expressed their frustration with what were apparently massive debts to local Jewish moneylenders. Increased taxation was coupled with poor harvests, the outbreak of disease, and for many, increased indebtedness to Jews.[48] According to Natalie Oeltjen, the concerns over baptism were secondary to the financial ones though the former were indeed supported by the clergy.

A group of peasants gathered outside the city of Majorca. Governor Francesc Sagarriga attempted to negotiate with the crowd, but he was attacked and wounded. The mob then proceeded to attack the royal castle at Bellver. They were unable to breach its walls. The crowd now turned its attention towards the Jewish quarter.

---

[46] Natalie Oeltjen, "Crisis and Regeneration: The Conversos of Majorca, 1391 - 1416."(PhD diss., University of Toronto, 2012), 5, 23.

[47] Cecil Roth, *A History of the Marranos* (Philadelphia: Jewish Publication Society, 1947), 12.

[48] Ibid., 12.

Several hundred Jews were killed, though the exact number is disputed.[49] Many Jews attempted to flee to North Africa while up to eight hundred Jews appear to have sought refuge in the royal castle. According to the historian Vicente Mut, the violence was primarily directed against Jews. Mut suggests that a Christian youth had died as a result of a confrontation with a young Jewish man. The Jew, merely trying to defend himself struggled with the man and killed him. The homes of Christian officials were then targeted since many of them were regarded as having protected Jews.[50] The violence continued, and the governor was still besieged in the palace. On the 27th of August, possibly four thousand armed peasants surrounded the city walls again and continued doing so for a week. The municipal judges gave in to various demands, which included the banning of corrupt officials from holding public office, a reform of the government to include greater representation of the peasants, the abolition of taxes, and the dismissal of all debts including those to Jews.[51]

A rumor that the king had ordered the execution of those sent by the peasants to negotiate on their behalf sparked another rebellion. On October 2nd, six to seven thousand armed men returned to the royal castle and besieged it. The mob issued a list of demands, which

---

[49] Natalie Oeltjen, "Crisis and Regeneration: The Conversos of Majorca, 1391 - 1416."(PhD diss., University of Toronto, 2012), 18.

[50] Cecil Roth, *A History of the Marranos* (Philadelphia: Jewish Publication Society, 1947), 20.

[51] Yitzhak Baer, *A History of the Jews in Christian Spain Volume 2* (Philadelphia: Jewish Publication Society, 1961), 102.

included that within eight days all the Jews who had sought refuge in the castle convert to Christianity or be killed.

The Jews agreed to the demand of conversion once the judges promised to pay 20,000 pounds of their corporate debt. According to Oeltjen, the judges were desperate to convince Jews to convert so that the peasants would be placated. With few options, around October 21st, the Jews in the castle converted.[52] In 1392, the island received a blanket amnesty for the attack on the Jewish quart er.

On Saturday, August 5th, the violence spread to Barcelona. On the first day, approximately 100 Jews were killed while several others found protection in a local fort. On the following day, the masses invaded the Jewish quarter and began looting. The authorities tried to protect the Jews, but a mob attacked them and freed those who had been imprisoned. The citadel was stormed on the 8th, and more than 300 Jews were murdered, including the only son of the famed Rabbi Ḥasdai ibn Crescas. Many Jews submitted to baptism as a way to escape the violence as the riot continued in Barcelona until August 10th. The Jewish quarter in Gerona was also attacked. While some fled, others were either killed or baptized.

---

[52] Natalie Oeltjen, "Crisis and Regeneration: The Conversos of Majorca, 1391 – 1416" (PhD diss., University of Toronto, 2012), 20-23.

On August 13th, the last town to experience an onslaught of violence was Lerida. The Jews of this city attempted to find safety in Alcazar. Seventy-five Jews were killed, and the rest were baptized. In Lerida, the municipal authorities asked the king to send someone to deal with the situation. The officials related that several monks had asked permission to enter the Jewish quarter with the purpose of preaching Christianity to Jews. The king denied their request.[53]

---

[53] Yitzhak Baer, *A History of the Jews in Christian Spain: Volume 2* (Philadelphia: Jewish Publication Society, 1961), 108.

CHAPTER 6

The Aftermath

Howard Sachar estimates that as many as 30,000 Jews died in the violence of 1391.[54] Cecil Roth mentions the death toll may have been as high as 50,000.[55] The severity of the persecutions, which led to the forced conversions, is related by Reuven, the son of the Rabbi Nissim Gerundi and a survivor of the massacre. He claimed that 140,000 Jews converted.[56] Salo Wittmayer Baron characterized the violence as a "holy war" against Judaism. Approximately a third of the Jewish population of the kingdoms of Castile and Aragon may have been massacred; a third escaped their attackers by temporarily fleeing their homes, and another third possibly converted to Christianity.[57] Communities,

---

[54] Howard Sachar, *Farewell Espana: The World of the Sephardim Remembered* (New York: Vintage Books, 1995), 44-45.

[55] Cecil Roth, *the Spanish Inquisition,* (New York: W.W. Norton and Company, 1964), 22.

[56] David Nirenberg, "Mass conversion and Genealogical Mentalities: Jews and Christians in Fifteenth-Century Spain," *Past and Present,* No. 174 (2002): 9.

[57] Salo Wittmayer Baron, *A Social and the Religious History of the Jews: Volume XI* (Philadelphia: Jewish Publication Society, 1967),

which had existed for centuries, were decimated, and tens of thousands of Jews were slaughtered.[58] Perhaps up to two hundred thousand Jews were forced to convert as a means to save their lives and the lives of their families.[59]

Four years later, Ferrant Martinez was incarcerated in Seville in 1395 by order of King Henry III but was rapidly released. Any concern which King Henry III felt over the destruction of the Jewish quarter of Seville was quickly forgotten. In 1396, he presented the Jewish quarter, including all its houses, lands, and synagogue buildings to two supporters. They were granted authority to sell, pledge as collateral, exchange, demolish, or otherwise administer this property according to their prerogative. The Jewish quarter was renamed the *Villa Nueva*. Its synagogues were converted into churches.

p.232. See also Kevin Ingram, "Secret lives, public lies: the conversos and socio-religious non-conformism in the Spanish Golden Age" (PhD diss., UC San Diego, 2006), 43-44.

[58] Cecil Roth, *A History of the Marranos* (Philadelphia: Jewish Publication Society, 1947), 12.

[59] Ibid., 13.

Conversos celebrating Passover secretly in Spain by Moshe Maimon

The remaining Jews continued to live in the old Jewish quarter and other areas. Due to the loss of tax revenue resulting from the decimation of the Jewish community, the city council granted permission to Jews to resume their traditional occupations. The situation remained precarious enough for the remaining Jews to hire 300 guards to protect them.

After the tragedy of 1391, hatred towards Jews continued to mount. The newly converted Jews known as *Conversos* were forbidden from sailing to Muslim lands.[60] Growing anti-Jewish legislation resulted in the emigration of many Jews from Castile and their relocation to the areas of Malaga, Almeria, and Granada where they were well received. The Jews of Córdoba were again attacked, and many of them murdered in 1406. King Henry III

---

[60] Yitzhak Baer, *A History of the Jews in Christian Spain: Volume 2* (Philadelphia: Jewish Publication Society, 1961), 102.

prohibited Jews from dressing like Christians. He also insisted on Jews wearing distinctive insignia. King Henry III died in 1406. In his will, Pablo de Santa Maria, the voluntary Jewish convert to Christianity was designated as executor of his will and protector of his son, John. The Regency was placed under the control of the Queen Mother Catalina and the *Infante* Fernando de Antequera.

Attempts to reestablish Jewish quarters, such as those in Barcelona or Valencia, were utter failures. The number of *Juderias* across the Kingdoms of Castile and Aragon in the 15th century was 216 and 35, respectively. Many of these were small and reflected the new reality of Jews having fled and abandoned the cities in favor of the countryside to prevent a population concentration, which had made them easier targets in previous years.

The theological challenges presented by the Conversos who continued to live alongside their Jewish compatriots were coupled with an economic transformation. The economic roles that Jews had typically filled were now increasingly occupied by Conversos. The hatred, which targeted Jews for usury and their roles as tax farmers, was steadily transferred to Conversos. Conversos were freed from the legal restrictions that had characterized their former status as Jews. These new opportunities included posts in public offices. As Converso prominence and services to the Crown grew, the relevance of the Jewish community lessened.

CHAPTER 7

Conversos among Jews and Christians

A mong Jews, these individuals, who converted under coercion or threat, were known as *anusim*, i.e. forced ones. Those who converted wholeheartedly and typically independent of any persecution were known as *meshumadim*, meaning 'he who destroys.'[61] Many of those who did convert did observe

---

[61] The 15th century polemical work, titled *El Alborayque*, provides a definition of the term Converso: "Deos tales neophitos o conuersos judayzantes es el presente tratado, y por este vocabo conersos no se entiendad todos aquellos que descienden de la generacion delos judios:alos quales el vulgo impropriamente llama conuersos: mas entiend<n> se solame<n>te los judios q<ue> se co<n>uertiero<n> xp<ist>ianos los q<ua>les conuersos judayza<n>tes como fuessen conuertidos mas por fuerca q<ue> de buena voluntad. (Fols 1v-2r)." According to this statement, only those Jews who sincerely converted to Christianity should be deemed Conversos—not those who were converted by force. Dwayne E. Carpenter "From Al-Burak to Alboraycos: The Art of Transformation on the Eve of the Expulsion" in *Jews and Conversos at the Time of the Expulsion*, edited by Yom Tov Assis, Yosef Kaplan. (Jerusalem: The Zalman Shazar Center for Jewish History, 1999),

Judaism clandestinely and were derogatorily called Judaizers or *Marranos* i.e. swine.[62] The term *Conversos* was also applied to their descendants who were not first generation converts but rather the descendants of practicing Jews (i.e. children, grandchildren, etc.) who had converted to Christianity in the late fourteenth and early fifteenth centuries.[63] This term was used in official correspondence.[64] By the middle of the sixteenth century,

---

32. Also Kevin Ingram, "Secret lives, public lies: the conversos and socio-religious non-conformism in the Spanish Golden Age" (PhD diss., UC San Diego, 2006), 1.

[62] The term *Marrano* has often been used to designate Conversos who converted to Christianity for survival sake and continued to observe Jewish practices in some form. The exact origins of the term are disputed, however. The famous Spanish dictionary of 1611 authored by Sebastián de Covarrubias defined the term Marrano as "*Es el rezien convertido al christianismo, tenemos ruin concepto del por averse convertido fingidamente.*" "The recent convert to Christianity, of whom we have a despicable opinion for having feigned his conversion." Diego Velazquez, the author of the pamphlet *Defensio Statuti Toletani* stated "*Sed eos hispani marranos vocare solemus, qui ex iudaeis descendentes et baptizati ficti christiani.*" "We call those Spaniards, Marranos, who are descendants of Jews and were baptized fictitiously as Christians." See Sebastian de Covarrubias Horozco, "Tesoro de la Lengua Castellana o Española [1611]" (Madrid: Ed. Turner, 1979).

[63] Miriam Bodian states: "The group was self-perpetuating, since descendants continued to be regarded as conversos, or converts, for many generations. And the ranks of this group grew... [...] The status of Converso became, curiously, and inherited status- a fateful development." Miriam Bodian, "'Men of the Nation': The Shaping of Converso Identity in Early Modern Europe," Past and Present 143(1994): 48–76.

[64] In 1380, King John of Castile, as well as the Cortes of Soria banned the use of terms 'turncoats' and Marranos. Those who

other terms were used to designate Conversos. These terms included *gente del linaje* (those of this lineage), *esta gente* (this people), *esta generacion* (this generation or this lineage), *esta raza* (this race), and *los de la nacion* (those of the nation). As these terms reveal, an increasing emphasis was given to the perceived ethnic or racial characteristics of Conversos.[65]

The sheer number of those killed, as well as those who converted under duress, was so significant that few if any, Jews were unaffected. Close-knit families were often comprised of members who survived the massacres without converting and others who had acquiesced or been forced to convert. Continuing economic, cultural, and religious ties to Judaism characterized many Conversos. The lack of extensive doctrinal education in Christianity, given to Conversos, reinforced the reality that for most, conversion was an insincere act borne out of necessity.

---

used it were subject to a penalty of 300 maravedis and fifteen days in prison. Salo Wittmayer Baron, *A Social and the Religious History of the Jews: Volume XIII* (Philadelphia: Jewish Publication Society, 1969), 66.

[65] Miriam Bodian, *Hebrews of the Portuguese Nation* (Bloomington: Indiana University Press, 1997), 11. Portuguese terms corresponding to the Castilian terms used included: *Cristãos Novos, gente da nação,* and *homens da nação.* Ibid., 12.

The Valencian Dominican friar, Vicente Ferrer by Giovanni Bellini

Vicente Ferrer, who had participated in the onslaught of the Jewish communities in 1391 by eagerly accepting Jews at baptismal fonts was convinced that the path forward was to instruct the remaining Jews in the reality of the Christian faith. With what must have been nothing less than dramatic confrontations, Ferrer journeyed the countryside with a Torah scroll in one hand and a cross in the other, preaching Christianity to Jews.[66] His zeal

---

[66] Cecil Roth, *A History of the Marranos* (Philadelphia: Jewish Publication Society, 1947), 13. Four thousand Jews are said to have converted on a single day in Toledo. In the Bishopric of Segovia, the surviving Jewish remnants were further devastated. So successful was Vicente Ferrer and his assistant Geronimo de Santa Fe, that large numbers of Jews from the cities of Saragossa, Calatayud, Daroca, Fraga, and Barbastro converted. The

was recognized by Pope Benedict XIII, who sought to appoint him as his confessor. However, Ferrer was driven by the goal of converting the remaining Jews.[67]

Ferrer rejected violence as a means of conversion, but his tactics were intimidating. With the violence of 1391 fresh in their minds, more Jews converted. This time, it had the official endorsement of the Castilian court. Rabbi Joseph ben Joshua ben Meir described Vicente Ferrer with the following statement:

> "He was unto them a Satan [adversary] and stirred up against them all the inhabitants of the country, and they arose to swallow them up alive and slew many with the edge of the sword, and many they burned with fire, and many they turned away with the power of the sword from the L-RD, the G-d of Israel. And they burned the books of the Law of our G-d, and trampled upon them the mire in the streets: and the mother they dashed in pieces

communities Alcaniz, Caspe, Maella, Lerida, Tamarit, and Alcolea converted on mass. Within a short period of time, 35,000 Jews were reported to have converted.

[67] A description of Vicente Ferrer is provided in the *Cronica de Los Reyes Catolicos* authored by Hernando del Pulgar, the royal historiographer to Queen Isabella and King Ferdinand. "A Catholic saint, a male doctor of the Dominican Order, which desired at that time by preaching... by the Holy Law and Scripture to convert all Jews from Spain, and to end the inveterate and stench ridden synagogue." Rica Amran Cohen, "Judíos y conversos en las crónicas de los Reyes de Castilla (desde finales del siglo XIV hasta la expulsión)," Espacio, Tiempo y Forma. Serie III. Historia medieval 9 (1996): 269.

upon her children in the day of the L-RD's wrath…"[68]

Vicente Ferrer and the Jewish Community

Ferrer traveled across Murcia, Lorca, Ocaña, Illescas, Valladolid, Tordesillas, Salamanca, and Zamora preaching. In July 1411, he reached Toledo where he took control of the main synagogue, which he converted into the Church of Santa Maria la Blanca. He reportedly baptized more than 4,000 Jews in Toledo. The less violent nature of the intimidation provoking these conversions is in contrast to the conversions experienced in 1391. Jews were certainly aware of the violence that erupted in Córdoba in 1406. Many may have seen Ferrer's actions as a prelude to another wave of violence. Taking control of the synagogue must have certainly required a mob or armed force of some kind.

---

[68] Henry Charles Lea, "Ferrand Martinez and the Massacres of 1391," The American Historical Review, Vol. 1. No. 2 (1896): 218.

The Synagogue of Toledo converted to the Church of Santa Maria la Blanca

With the help of the Converso Pablo de Santa Maria, Ferrer pushed through legislation aimed at curtailing Jewish social, economic, and religious freedom. Several laws were enacted on January 1412 under the auspices of King John II. Furthermore, Jews were prohibited from practicing medicine and ordered to isolate themselves socially in designated Jewish quarters. Ferrer explained that "Just as prostitutes should live apart, so should Jews."[69] Failing to comply within eight days of the decree would result in property loss. They were also banned from selling bread, wine, flour, and meat and from almost every economic activity. Holding public office and acting as money brokers were also forbidden. Regarding the intensity of the anti-Jewish legislation, Rabbi Solomon Alami wrote:

> "They barred us from commerce, agriculture, and crafts. They forced us to grow beards and hair long. Former palace dwellers were driven into wretched hovels and ill-lit huts. Instead of the rustle of silk, we were compelled to wear miserable clothing that only drew further contempt and revulsion upon us. Hunger looked everyone in the face, and children died at their mothers' breast from exposure and starvation."[70]

They were also restricted from eating and drinking with Christians or hiring them as servants. Practically all social interaction with Christians was prohibited.[71] Christian women, married or unmarried, were forbidden to enter the Jewish quarter, either by day or night. Even the ability to levy communal taxes was prohibited without royal permission. Markings of social rank, such as the title *Don,* were prohibited as was their ability to bear weapons. Men and women were also required to wear distinctive clothes consisting of long plain mantles of coarse material reaching the feet. Leaving the country

---

[69] Howard Sachar, *Farewell Espana: The World of the Sephardim Remembered* (New York: Vintage Books, 1995), 50.

[70] Ibid., 51.

[71] Ibid., 51.

to follow Jewish life unrestrained by Castilian rule, or even changing residences was prohibited and punishable by loss of property and even slavery.[72]

Ferrer's zeal was not limited to Castile. He continued undisturbed in Aragon. The *Infante* Fernando de Antequera had recently ascended to the throne in part through the machinations of Ferrer. In 1407, King Henry III died leaving the throne of Castile to his young son. His wife and brother Fernando served as regents. In 1410, the King of Aragon also died, but without leaving a successor. Fernando vied for the throne of Aragon, and Vicente Ferrer's support was apparently essential to the former's goal of assuming the Aragonese crown. Perhaps with this in mind, he acted to implement a series of anti-Jewish laws in January 1412.[73] The same month Fernando received support for his goal and was to be installed as King of Aragon the following year. Ferrer's campaign of intimidation led many Jews to adopt Christianity in the cities of Saragossa, Daroco, and Calatayud. Other conversions occurred in Albacete, Astorga, Avila, Benevent, Burgos, Leon, Mayorga, Majorca, Palencia, Paredes, Toro, and Segovia. Vicente Ferrer's attempt to extend his campaign into Portuguese territory was abruptly halted by King John I of Portugal.[74]

---

[72] Ibid., 51.

[73] Fernando Suárez Bilbao, *Cristianos Contra Judíos y Conversos* (Madrid : Universidad «Rey Juan Carlos», 2004), 462.

[74] Salo Wittmayer Baron, *A Social and the Religious History of the Jews: Volume X* (Philadelphia: Jewish Publication Society, 1965), 163.

The Tortosa Disputation

The new laws adopted at Ayllon changed the relationship with the Jewish communities of Castile. The goal was to apply sufficient pressure for Jews to convert to Christianity. This was to be accomplished by reinforcing the restrictions on them. The Converso Geronimo de Santa Fe appealed for the Pope's consent to resolve the Jewish question definitively. The plan envisioned the collapse of rabbinic authority and legitimacy. The Pope agreed to Sante Fe's plan. In November 1412, the *aljamas* of Aragon were summoned to provide their representatives to Tortosa on January 15th, 1413, where they would be presented with irrefutable proof that Jesus was, indeed, the true Messiah. If the rabbis were shown the error of their ways and if they would submit to baptism, then surely the rest of the Jewish community would follow.

The rabbis who attended had little choice in the matter. The Tortosa affair lasted almost two years. Pope Benedict XIII clearly stipulated that this was not a debate, but rather an opportunity to reveal the Biblical and Talmudic evidence that confirmed the messianic claims of Christianity. Fernando Suarez Bilbao describes it as a dialogue of the deaf where the rabbis did not understand Christian syllogisms and the Christians did not comprehend the rabbis. [75]

[75] Fernando Suárez Bilbao, *Cristianos Contra Judíos y Conversos* (Madrid: Universidad «Rey Juan Carlos», 2004), 463.

The representatives of the Jewish community who attended the disputation included a large number of prominent individuals.[76] The pope presided at the first meeting, which occurred before an audience of more than a thousand people. The disputation was led by Geronimo de Santa Fé and another Converso Garci Alvarez de Alarcon and the theologian Andreas Beltran of Valencia. The Jewish opposition was led by Vidal Benveniste. During the sixty-fifth session, Joseph Albo and Astruc ha-Levi presented a resolute defense of the Talmud, on November 10th,1414. Astruc ha-Levi, with the support of most of the Jewish representatives, declared that the aggadic passages were not regarded as authoritative by them.

In the summer of 1413 and the first six months of 1414, approximately 200 Jews from Saragossa, Calatayud, and Alcaniz acceded to baptism. Additional communities such as Guadalajara, Daroca, Fraga, Tamarite, Barbasto, Alcolea Caspe, and Maella also submitted to baptism. The historian Zurita relates that more than 3,000 Jews were baptized in 1414. Hoping to build on the growing number of conversions that had occurred, Pope Benedict issued a bull on May 11th, 1415. This edict corresponded with the *Pragmatica* decree issued by Catalonia and which had been adopted in Aragon by King Ferdinand. The

---

[76] These included Rabbi Mattityahu Hayitzhari, Rabbi Ferrer Saladin, and Rabbi Moses aben Abez. The philosopher Joseph Albo of Monreal, Astruc ha-Levi of Alcañiz, Bonjudah Yehasel Hakaslari, and Profet Duran were also present among others. Yitzhak Baer, *A History of the Jews in Christian Spain Volume 2* (Philadelphia: Jewish Publication Society, 1961), 173.

order prohibited Jews and Conversos from studying the Talmud, reading anti-Christian writings, manufacturing communion cups or other church vessels or accepting either as pledges, building new synagogues or restoring old ones.[77]

Each community was allowed to have only one synagogue. Jews were also denied previously held rights of self-jurisdiction, and they were also not authorized to seek retribution against accusers. Jews were also barred from holding public offices. As they had experienced previously, they were prohibited from serving as brokers, matrimonial agents, physicians, or apothecaries.

On a more religiously focused side, Jews were forbidden to bake or sell unleavened bread for Passover. Should their children become Christians, Jews were also prohibited from disinheriting them. They were to wear the distinctive badge at all times, and three times a year all those over the age of twelve were forced to listen to Christian sermons on the Messiah.[78]

---

[77] Amia Raphael. Jewish Virtual Library, "Goldsmiths and Silversmiths." Last modified 2008 – accessed July 31, 2015 http://www.jewishvirtuallibrary.org/jsource/judaica/ejud_0002_0 007_0_07579.html. See also Yitzhak Baer, *A History of the Jews in Christian Spain Volume 2* (Philadelphia: Jewish Publication Society, 1961), 229.

[78] "That in all cities, towns, and villages, where there may be the number of Jews the diocesan may deem sufficient, three public sermons are to be preached annually; one on the second Sunday in Advent; one on the festival of the Resurrection; and the other on the Sunday when the Gospel, 'And Jesus approached Jerusalem,' is chanted. All Jews above twelve years of age shall be compelled to

Rabbis like Joseph Albo, a Jewish philosopher and author of *Sefer ha-Ikkarim* and others remained spiritually and intellectually committed to the survival of Judaism. King Ferdinand I of Aragon died in April 1416 and his successor King Alfonso V declared that he would not put the Papal Bull of 1415 into effect. The final solution to the Jewish dilemma was postponed for another time. In 1418, Martin V arrived as a representative of papal authority. He severely prohibited conversions by force, a measure that may indicate that they were still being applied, either directly or indirectly.

The Jewish community felt sufficiently secure to request a formal rescinding of the 1415 Papal Bull via Jewish representatives sent to Rome. This request was granted in 1419. Despite relief from this edict, the day to day conditions of Jews remained tenuous. They were driven towards social and economic marginalization. This economic marginalization lessened their importance to the Crown, which in turn, translated into less pressure on the local authorities to ensure their protection.

A partial turn of fortunes in Castile was brought about in large part by the efforts of Abraham Benveniste.

---

attend to hear these sermons. The subjects are to be – the first, to show them that the true Messiah has already come, quoting the passages of the Holy Scripture and the Talmud that were argued in the disputation of Jerome of Santa Fe; the second, to make them see that the heresies, vanities and errors of the Talmud, prevent their knowing the truth; and the third, explaining to them the destruction of the Temple and the city of Jerusalem, and the perpetuity of their captivity, as our Lord Jesus Christ and the other prophets prophesied." Ibid.

Benveniste served as a courtier to King Juan II beginning in 1420. His financial acumen proved invaluable to Alvaro de Luna, who succeeded Juan II. In the war of 1429 against Aragon, Abraham Benveniste had supported Alvaro with the financial resources at his disposal. As compensation for his support, Alvaro reestablished the position of Chief Rabbi of all Jewish communities and named him to the post. With it, the Jews of Castile regained a measure of their former glory. He restored the practice whereby representatives of the Jewish communities journeyed to the city in which the Cortes had convened with the acknowledgment of the King. Benveniste exploited his relationship with the King to accomplish a new chapter in the history of Iberian Jewry. From the 25th of April through to the 5th of May 1432 Jewish representatives from the various communities of Castile gathered along with several Jewish courtiers in the city of Valladolid.

Under the direction of Benveniste, several *takkanot* (religious edicts) for the Jewish communities in Castile were issued. The key, however, was the fact that they were presented to the King for review and authorization. What may have seemed to be a mere ceremonial act effectively legitimatized the Jewish community, its laws, and its ability to self-govern. It restored a measure of Jewish autonomy, which mirrored that offered to other citizens and marked the first time a European monarch had ratified a Jewish law derived and deliberated exclusively by Jews. Benveniste offered a radical alternative to those who sought a resolution to the Jewish question by conversion or expulsion. Instead, the legitimacy and loyalty of the Jewish community could be recognized as a component of Castilian life and identity. This model, which saw Jews as members of a distinct religion, was not only based on the Torah, which Christians recognized but on the very Talmud that had previously proved the source of so much condemnation. Among the ordinances passed, were directives stipulating the educational responsibilities that rested on *aljamas* according to their size. The nature of the education which included Talmudic instruction was undoubtedly well known to the Crown. Benveniste's actions secured the Jewish communities of Castile a degree of autonomy. Even though it did not match that achieved during the 13th century, it certainly provided the stability necessary to begin the process of recovery in the aftermath of the physical violence and theological attacks of the previous forty years.[79]

The continued Jewish practices of many Conversos, their ongoing family, and Jewish cultural ties, coupled with the fact that the Old Christians were well aware that their conversions had occurred under coercion created an environment of suspicion. The success of many Conversos only added to the resentment. Many Conversos had entered into the army. Some had taken administrative positions in local government; a number studied law while others entered the universities. Some even joined the Church. Conversos were eventually found at the highest positions at court.[80]

---

[79] Fernando Suárez Bilbao, *Cristianos Contra Judíos y Conversos* (Madrid: Universidad «Rey Juan Carlos», 2004), 466-467.

[80] Cecil Roth, *A History of the Marranos* (Philadelphia: Jewish Publication Society, 1947), 14.

The financial success of many Conversos has been viewed as the primary motivator of anti-Converso sentiment. However, the religious undertones were always present. Christian anti-Judaism had an established history whose influence was not decoupled from Conversos simply by the fact that they had formally adopted Christianity. What had once been a Jewish problem was now being transformed into a Converso one with many clamoring for the separation of these New Christians just as they had done towards Jews. The motivation behind this was the seeming restoration of Iberian Judaism, which was drawing Conversos back to the fold. The recovery of the religious, intellectual, and moral life of the Jewish community was sufficiently strong to attract converts to return to their former religion, thus creating a dangerous infiltration into Christian society.[81]

In 1449, 1467, 1470, and 1473, violence broke out against Conversos. While financial considerations were part of the concern, Judaizing was also an essential element. The need to establish royal authority was evident to both Jews and Conversos alike.[82] The crisis of who would succeed King Juan II of Castile led to a division among the nobility. Princess Juana's claim to the throne of Castile gained the support of Juan Fernández Pacheco, the Marquez of Villena—a powerful political operative. The violence and chaos provided him with the opportunity to get control of the city of Segovia. Two

---

[81] Fernando Suárez Bilbao, *Cristianos Contra Judíos y Conversos* (Madrid: Universidad «Rey Juan Carlos», 2004), 471.

[82] Ibid., 473.

individuals, the Converso Andres Cabrera and Abraham Seneor, the chief tax-farmer, colluded to take control of the city and present it to Princess Isabella along with access to the Alcazar and the royal treasure. In return for their loyalty, Andres Cabrera was named Marquez of Moya and Abraham Seneor as Chief Rabbi. He also served as the royal tax farmer and the *Alguacil Mayor* of the *aljama* of Segovia.

The need to reestablish royal authority and quench the violence erupting against Jews and Conversos was entirely logical since it was for the benefit of the kingdom.[83] Both men believed that Isabella was best able to guarantee stability. The subsequent marriage of Ferdinand of Aragon and Isabella of Castile initiated a period of ten years, which were mostly marked by the well-being of the Jewish community and a return to order. This stability was soon to end, though. Converso critics pointed to the fact that not only untrustworthy Conversos were present at court, but that unconverted Jews had now re-entered the scene. In addition to Abraham Seneor, they could point to Vidal Astori, Meir Melamed, Samuel Abulafia, the grandsons of Abraham Benveniste, Abraham and Vidal, as well as the newly arrived Isaac Abravanel who would eventually rise as the leader of the Castilian Jewish community.

While the rise of these influential Jewish courtiers hearkened back to earlier days of seeming Jewish integration, the real life conditions of Jews was quite different. Royal protection granted to Jewish

---

[83] Ibid., 474.

communities was often ineffectual. The towns and villages home to Jews were increasingly resistant to recommendations initiated by the royal counsel. The stability of Jewish communities of Castile and Aragon was increasingly fragile. The complexity of the Jewish situation was reflected by the fact that many Jews had reentered the royal court where their position and influence on royal dispositions towards the Jewish community were of paramount significance. Their service to the court increased the stability of the kingdom and strengthened the monarch's hand. Nevertheless, the socio-economic status of the majority of Jews ultimately diminished the importance of Jewish communities for the Crown. By the 1480s, many Jews were often small merchants selling dried fish, shoemakers, and vendors of used clothing, pawnbrokers, jewelers, and the like. Jewish farmers, typically rare due to restrictions on land ownership and usages, were also present. The fanciful image of the powerful Jew critical to the financial well-being of the state, an image always exaggerated, had eroded.

CHAPTER 8

A Shared Destiny

The continued Jewish presence was seen by individuals such as Fray Alonso de Espina and others as destructive and as a potential virus that was spreading among Conversos and could even infect Old Christians. Relentlessly, they sought to persuade Pope Sixtus IV that the reality of secret Jewish practices was both widespread and dangerous. The solution to the problem was the invigoration and intensification of the Inquisitorial process, which technically had been authorized under the reign of King Enrique IV, but had either not been implemented or was ineffectual. In October 1477, Nicolas Franco, the papal legate initiated important discussions with King Ferdinand of Aragon and Queen Isabella of Castile in the city of Seville. Ferdinand and Isabella convinced the Pope that the control of the Inquisitorial process should be conceded to the Crown under the direction of the Dominicans and the secular authorities who would administer punishment. Whatever regret the Pope would later express towards the effective transfer of Papal power to the Crown, the new Inquisition was then unleashed in a manner that was far different from the earlier Papal Inquisitions.[84]

The Establishment of the Inquisition

The new Inquisition in contrast to the earlier Papal Inquisitions was focused on the stated purpose of rooting out Judaizing among Conversos. Only later would both Inquisitions redirect their attention to *Moriscos* – Muslim converts to Christianity – who continued to practice Islam clandestinely, early Protestantism, witchcraft, bigamy, etc. Both institutions

[84] The *Cronica de los Reyes Catolicos* authored by Hernando Pulgar relates that, "Some clerics and religious people and many other lay people informed King and the Queen, that in their kingdoms and lordships there were many Christians of the lineage of the Jews, who were Judaizing, and practicing Jewish rites secretly at home, and had not believed the Christian faith or works that Catholic Christians were supposed to observe. This known by the King and Queen, they expressed great regret, to see people who were not loyal to the Catholic Faith and were heretics and apostates ... Fray Tomas de Torquemada... placed inquisitors in all the cities and villages ... the Kingdoms of Castile and they placed them in his letters of edicts, founded by law, so that those who had Judaized or were not loyal to the faith were allowed to confess their sins within a certain time, and be reconciled to the Holy mother Church ... From these were burned at different times and in some cities and villas, two thousand men and women ... These were especially from Seville and Cordoba, and the cities and villages of Andalusia where four thousand homes were to be found and many of this lineage lived there and they left the land with their wives and children." Rica Amran Cohen, "Judíos y conversos en las crónicas de los Reyes de Castilla (desde finales del siglo XIV hasta la expulsión)," Espacio, Tiempo y Forma. Serie III. Historia medieval 9 (1996): 267

would arrest and try Conversos for Judaizing in the Iberian Peninsula, as well as throughout Spanish and Portuguese colonies across the world well into the 18th century.

Inquisition in Terreiro do Paco, Lisbon

Among the first moves of the Inquisition in the city of Seville was the forced relocation of Jewish communities to ensure that Jews and Christians were separated. Fray Miguel de Morillo ordered the relocation of the Jewish quarter to the Corral de Jerez, a smaller and squalid area. The move was sanctioned by Queen Isabella cloaked with guarantees of safety and security. The onset of this new empowered Inquisition appears to have kindled others ready to act on the unresolved place of Jews in Spain. In 1480, the Cortes assembled in Toledo where anti-Jewish regulations, dating back to 1412, were reissued. Two years were allotted for all Jewish quarters to be relocated far away from the center of the city. Each was to be furnished with walls and gates under watch. Both monarchs consented to the petition. Jewish business activity was curtailed. The forced move of Jews from one section of the city to another also caused financial difficulties for those who had to sell their houses at relatively low prices.

The inquisitors, if nothing else, were diligent in their work as they proceeded to collect information on Judaizers. They argued to the monarchs that the number of Judaizers was in the thousands. While they could punish Conversos, who relapsed into Judaism, the heart of the problem lay in the continued Jewish presence in the infected areas. The Inquisitor General, Miguel de Morillo, requested that the Jews be expelled from the principal cities of Andalusia including Seville, Cadiz, and Córdoba. The royal council ratified the move and Jews were given six months to vacate the area. The expulsion of Jews from the region of Andalusia was the first expulsion edict issued in the Peninsula.[85]

That expulsion impacted the neighboring kingdom of Portugal, where a burst of violence erupted in 1482 when a mob attacked several Jews. Jewish-owned stores and homes were destroyed in Lisbon. In the ensuing rampage, Don Isaac Abravanel lost his entire belongings

---

[85] "... all... wanted to rid the land of this sin of heresy, because [they] understood that this was G-d's and his service." Yolanda Quesada Morillas "La expulsión de los judíos andaluces a finales del siglo xv y suprohibición de pase a Indias," Actas del I Congreso Internacional sobre Migraciones en Andalucía (2011): 2100.

including his precious library. The infamous epidemic of the Black Death also broke out concurrently with the arrival of the Jewish refugees from Castile. The city council ordered that all *émigrés* were to vacate the city immediately. Only two notables, Samuel Nayas, the Procurator of Castilian Jewry and the Castilian physician Samuel Judah, were allowed to remain and only through the intervention of King John II.

Many Jews believed the measures were temporary, and would continue only as long as the Inquisitional tribunals lasted. Before the courts initiated their proceedings, some Conversos had already abandoned the cities and escaped to the Castilian region of Extremadura, the Kingdom of Portugal, or the Kingdom of Granada.[86] Others sought refuge under the protection of the archbishops. The tribunals were in full swing with thousands of suspected Judaizers arrested and tortured and hundreds, if not thousands, sentenced to burn at the stake as unrepentant apostates.[87] As the courts expanded their reach to other

---

[86] Ibid.

[87] The Cronica de los Reyes Catolicos written by Hernando del Pulgar states the following. "... [they] were and were still secret Jews, and were neither Jews nor Christians but they were baptized and were heretics.... they refused to eat pork unless they were forced, they ate beef ...and secretly kept the Passover and Saturdays as best they could, they sent to synagogues oil lamps, Jews preached to them at home in secret, especially to the women; they were very secret rabid Jews whose cattle and poultry were slaughtered at their businesses; they ate unleavened bread at the appropriate time, ... they made all the Jewish ceremonies in secret, so the men and the women always excused themselves from receiving the sacraments of the Holy Church ... except by force in accordance with the ordinances of the Church." Rica Amran

cities, the argument for segregation and expulsion intensified.

While thousands were burned, the Inquisitors continued to argue for their final solution to the root of the heresy. In 1490, their efforts were given a significant boost. The event was known as the incident of the *Santo Niño de la Guardia*. Jews and Conversos were accused of orchestrating the ritual murder of a Christian boy, profaning Christian symbols, and performing black magic in the process. It was no matter that the name of the boy, who was purportedly murdered, was not identified. The purported Jewish influence on Conversos was highlighted as another example of the danger the former's presence constituted.[88]

The drive against Jews was overshadowed by the final push against the last Muslim kingdom in Spain. The war against the Kingdom of Granada required support from all facets of Castilian and Aragonese society, including the valuable contributions of Jews. The need to maintain Jewish support was evidenced by King Ferdinand's refusal to implement an order in Aragon similar to that executed in Andalusia. Both monarchs had also guaranteed the property rights of those Jews forced to move from Andalusia. Jewish courtiers probably had sufficient reason for believing that their situation was not as unstable as it may have seemed. The success of the

---

Cohen, "Judíos y conversos en las crónicas de los Reyes de Castilla (desde finales del siglo XIV hasta la expulsión)," Espacio, Tiempo y Forma. Serie III. Historia medieval 9 (1996): 269- 270.

[88] Fernando Suárez Bilbao, *Cristianos Contra Judíos y Conversos* (Madrid: Universidad «Rey Juan Carlos», 2004), 479.

war in 1492 and the ongoing dilemma of Conversos and Judaizing appears to have resolved the matter. On March 20th, the new Chief Inquisitor, Tomas de Torquemada, presented the monarchy with the plan for the complete expulsion of Jews and on the 31st of March, the edict was published in Granada. The need for the Expulsion was rationalized as due to the failure of the Inquisition.[89]

The decree had an immediate effect. The Chief Rabbi, Abraham Seneor, converted. The defection of Seneor was devastating. Isaac Abravanel attempted to change the minds of both Ferdinand and Isabella and apparently, came close to achieving it. In the end, any hope for Spanish Jews to remain in the kingdoms of Castile and Aragon was crushed. Those Jews who fled to Portugal or Navarre soon faced a similar situation, only a few years later. The Inquisition remained focused on suspected Judaizers for years to come, reinforced by converted Jews in Portugal, as well as those Conversos who managed to escape to the various domains of the Spanish and Portuguese empires. The Chronicler Andres Bernaldez relates that the Spanish monarchs decided to expel Jews from Spain to put an end to the Mosaic heresy.[90] Some of the Jews who managed to flee Spain journeyed to Sicily and Naples, territories under or eventually under the control of King Ferdinand. Having

---

[89] Yolanda Quesada Morillas "La expulsión de los judíos andaluces a finales del siglo xv y suprohibición de pase a Indias," Actas del I Congreso Internacional sobre Migraciones en Andalucía (2011): 2101-2102.

[90] Eleazar Gutwirth, "The Jews in 15th Century Castilian Chronicles," The Jewish Quarterly Review, LXXIV. No.4 (1984): 395.

escaped the Peninsula, many were overwhelmed by the possibility of another dangerous exit and opted for conversion.[91]

---

[91] In 1468, King Ferdinand was crowned King of Sicily and in 1503, he assumed control of the Kingdom of Naples. As Nadia Zeldes relates: "Most scholars now agree that between 15,000 and 20,000 exiles reached the kingdom of Naples in the aftermath of the expulsions from the Iberian Peninsula and Sicily. King Ferrante I welcomed all the new immigrants, but shortly after this death (January 1494), hostility towards the Jews broke out through the kingdom...At Lecce, the crowds cried: [Death, death to the Jews unless they become Christians]' forcing the Jews to choose between death and conversion. In light of these circumstances, many exiles opted for conversion and journeyed back to Sicily." Nadia Zeldes, "Legal Status of Jewish Converts to Christianity to Southern Italy and Provence," California Italian Studies Journal, Vol.1:1 (2010): 5, 9.

Expulsion of the Jews by Emili Sala Francés

In the other fateful event of 1492, Spanish exploration under Christopher Columbus discovered the New World. The "Indies" provided opportunities for those Jews and Conversos caught in the current state of affairs, but a series of prohibitions regarding Jewish and Converso settlement in the newly discovered territories was implemented. Immigrating to the New World required royal permission.

In 1493, Ferdinand and Isabella decreed that royal licenses were needed for anyone wishing to travel to the New World. Hence, any person planning a trip to the New World had to meet with the Admiralty with the purpose registering each traveler. In 1501, Fray Nicolas de Obando issued further instructions for obtaining the royal license. Those wanting to travel to the new World had to provide information regarding their lives and practices to the "Tribunal de la Casa de Contratacion," which started issuing licenses as of 1503. The request for a permit was made to the court. While the majority of individuals were selected for a particular role based on their experience, permission was not granted to Moors, Jews, heretics, Gypsies, individuals reconciled by the Inquisition, or those recently converted to the Catholic faith.[92] Concerning those Jews who chose to leave, some

---

[92] For additional information see Yolanda Quesada Morillas "La expulsión de los judíos andaluces a finales del siglo xv y suprohibición de pase a Indias," Actas del I Congreso Internacional sobre Migraciones en Andalucía (2011): 2099, 2102-2104.

of them faced severe challenges along the way and therefore decided to return to the Peninsula and submit to the possible scrutiny of the Inquisition, as well as the increasing *Limpieza de Sangre* prohibitions being adopted.

CHAPTER 9

The Forced Conversions in Portugal

Following the expulsion orders of Castile and Aragon, the king of Portugal allowed Jewish refugees to reside in his kingdom for eight months in return for payment. He agreed to provide them with sufficient ships to carry them to their final destinations. The exact numbers of émigrés are difficult to confirm, but possibly up to 100,000 Jews entered Portugal from Castile. King John II did not keep his pledge, however. Some ships were provided, but the circumstances under which they arrived were terrible. Anyone who remained in the kingdom after the approved period was enslaved. King John also ordered that children be taken from parents who refused to convert. Some were sent to the recently discovered island of St. Thomas. Most of these died in route or from the severe conditions on the island.[93]

---

[93] Jane S. Gerber, *The Jews of Spain* (New York: The Free Press, 1992), 141.

After King John's death, his cousin and brother-in-law Manuel was crowned king of Portugal. He ruled from 1495-1521. King Manuel granted freedom to those who had been enslaved. His marriage to the daughter of King Ferdinand and Queen Isabella radically changed the situation, however. King Ferdinand and Queen Isabella conceded to the wedding on the condition that King Manuel expel all the Jews from his territory.[94]

On December 4th, 1496, King Manuel issued the edict of expulsion. All Jews were ordered to leave the kingdom of Portugal by the end of October 1497. Failure to do so was punishable by death and confiscation of their property. The king allowed Jews to depart with all their property. Desperate to keep Jews from leaving the country, he ordered that all Jewish children between the ages of four to fourteen be taken from their parents and brought up as Christians. They were to be permanently separated from their parents if the latter rejected conversion. The forced baptisms were scheduled to start on the first day of the Passover, Sunday, March 19th. Some parents killed their children to prevent them from being baptized. The Portuguese king, much more concerned with the long-term economic impact their exit would pose, opted for a very different strategy than his Spanish counterparts. The king ordered that all remaining Jews were to go to Lisbon to board their waiting ships. They were informed that the time allocated for their departure had lapsed. As a consequence, they were now the king's slaves. They were induced to convert to Christianity, but this failed. The king then

---

[94] Ibid., 141-142.

ordered his agents to use force. Many were dragged into churches and baptized.[95]

On May 30, 1497, the king introduced a law protecting baptized Jews. The law stated that baptized Jews were to be left unmolested for twenty years. The authorities could not accuse them of Judaizing during this period. When this time expired, any complaint related to Jewish observance would only result in a civil suit being brought against them. If the person in question was convicted, their property was to pass to their Christian inheritors and not into the fiscal treasury. The possession of Hebrew books was prohibited excepting Jewish physicians and surgeons who were permitted to consult Hebrew medical works.

Some Conversos managed to sell their property and emigrate. The numbers were apparently significant enough to merit royal concern. In April 1499, King Manuel prohibited business transactions by Conversos which involved bills of exchange or selling their real estate. They were forbidden to leave Portugal without royal authorization. Those who assisted them in fleeing was subject to punishment.[96]

As in Castile, the animosity directed towards Jews was quickly transferred to these Conversos. King Emanuel attempted to assuage these new converts with the hope

---

[95] Ibid., 142.

[96] Salo Wittmayer Baron, *A Social and the Religious History of the Jews: Volume XIII* (Philadelphia: Jewish Publication Society, 1969), 46.

that they would sincerely adopt the Christian faith. The ability of the king to shelter them against provocative speeches of zealous priests was limited, however.

On May 25th 1504, several Conversos met in the Rua Nova, the former *Juderia*. As they conversed, they were encircled by a pack of angry youths who affronted them. One of the Conversos drew his sword and wounded some of them. An uproar followed but was ultimately checked by the appearance of the governor of the city with an armed guard. Forty of the rioters were detained and convicted. They were flogged and were sentenced to banishment on the island of St. Thomas. The queen eventually interceded, and they were absolved.

This unrest was followed by the appalling massacre of Conversos in Lisbon two years later. A group of Conversos was attacked, and some Conversos were arrested, on the night of April 17, 1506. They were released after two days. The public was furious at their release and gossiped about bribery having secured their release. On April 19 another incident occurred when Old Christians and Conversos attended a Church service. Services were held to pray for the end of a devastating pestilence that had broken out. In a side chapel, a crucifix was reported to radiate an exceptional brilliance. This attracted the attention of Christians, who proclaimed it a miracle. A Converso voiced his lack of faith in the purported miracle sparking a riot.

Lisbon Massacre of 1506

The Converso was grabbed by the hair, dragged out of the building, and immediately killed by a mob. Two Dominican monks, Joaõ Mocho from the city of Evora, and Bernardo from the Kingdom of Aragonese paraded through the streets carrying a crucifix and shouting "heresy." They urged the people to eradicate all heretics. The fury of the crowds was added to by German, Dutch, and French sailors in port at the time. The result was a widespread slaughter. On the first day of the violence, over five hundred Conversos were murdered. At the end of the violence between 2,000 and 4,000 Conversos were killed the course of forty-eight hours.

The king responded by arresting and executing the ringleaders and others involved in the violence. The two Dominican monks participating in the unrest were expelled from their order and strangled. Any resident who was found guilty of either theft or homicide was punished corporally and lay open to loss of their property. Friars who had taken part in the uprising were expelled from the monastery. Following the calamity some Conversos left the kingdom. Some apparently returned to Lisbon and for a time were sheltered by the King.

King Manuel also arranged new privileges to Conversos and issued an edict on March 1, 1507, allowing them to leave the country with their property. Those that stayed were also reassured by the renewal the law of May 30, 1497, protecting Conversos from inquisitorial prosecution. On April 21, 1512, it was prolonged for an additional period of twenty years. In 1521, emigration was again prohibited. Attempts to violate this ordinance resulted in the of confiscation of property and loss of freedom.[97]

---

[97] In 1524, King John accepted a reported presented by Jorge Themudo. The report presented information gathered from parish priests on the activities of Conversos in their area. The report summarized by the Portuguese historian Alexandre Herculano related that "...the New Christians ceased to attend divine service on Sundays and religious holidays; that they did not bury their dead in the parish churchyards;...that when close to the death they neither received nor asked for extreme unction.; that in their wills

Despite this, during the remainder of King Manuel's reign Conversos did not face further unrest. When King Manual died, his son John III ascended the throne. He ruled from 1521-1557. On December 17, 1531, Pope Clement VII sanctioned the introduction of the Inquisition into the kingdom of Portugal. Some Conversos left the country. This occurred particularly during the reign of King Sebastian who ruled from 1557-1578. King Sebastian allowed New Christians to legally emigrate as long as they paid the enormous sum of 250,000 ducats.

In 1580, the Spanish Crown seized the Kingdom of Portugal. This initially had a positive impact on Portuguese Conversos as various economic opportunities were open to them particularly in centers such as Seville and Madrid. The new political reality also provided some relief to Portuguese Conversos fleeing from the Portuguese Inquisition since they could not be tried in Spanish territory for purported crimes done in the Kingdom of Portugal. The Spanish Inquisition could try them for Judaizing on Castilian soil, however. Despite this, increased numbers of Portuguese Conversos journeyed to Castile where many of them became successful merchants and some even serving as

---

they never provided for masses to be said for their souls;…that they were suspected of observing Saturdays and the ancient Passover;…that they practiced acts of charity among themselves, but not toward the Old Christians;…[yet] they got married at church doors, and baptized their children, observing precisely all the customary rites and solemnities." Salo Wittmayer Baron, *A Social and the Religious History of the Jews: Volume XIII* (Philadelphia: Jewish Publication Society, 1969), 48.

prominent royal financiers. Portuguese Conversos became a focus of inquisitional queries, and the word Portuguese would increasingly become synonymous with the term Judaizer.[98]

---

[98] Miriam Bodian, *Hebrews of the Portuguese Nation* (Bloomington: Indiana University Press, 1997), 13.

CHAPTER 10

Conclusions

The Inquisition continued its campaign of targeting Conversos it believed were Judaizing. During the first forty years of the Holy Office's term, thousands of Conversos were burned at the stake with thousands more subject to protracted prison sentences and the confiscation of their property. After 1520, the focus of the Inquisition shifted towards other emerging threats with those accused of Judaizing representing only a small fraction of the total trials. This trend was interrupted by spells of activity particularly with the influx of Portuguese Conversos entering Spain in the late 16th and 17th centuries. The decline in prosecutions, however, has led many to believe that Conversos had integrated to the dominant Christian faith and culture.[99]

More likely, as Kevin Ingram suggests, is the rerouting of Converso energies. The major reform movements of the early modern period in Spain were led by Conversos or strongly supported by them. One of the best examples is the *Alumbrado* or the Illuminist movement. The

---

[99] Kevin Ingram, ed., *The Conversos and Moriscos in Late Medieval Spain and Beyond: Volume Two* (Leiden: Brill, 2012), 1.

practitioners of this mystical form of Christianity rejected Catholic dogma by refraining from external worship common to traditional Catholicism. They also regarded the sacraments as useless. This movement was filled with Conversos, who also gravitated towards political movements like the Comunero revolt of 1521. Converso craftsman and traders were disproportionately represented in this attack on the Crown, which had accumulated administrative power at the expense of the nobility and the aristocratic classes. Conversos, at the royal court and the universities, were also active in Spain's Erasmian movement. The reform movement entered the Iberian Peninsula in 1517 with the court of Charles I. The Erasmian humanistic movement provided Conversos with the opportunity to attack Catholic practices with cover. The trend continued until the 1530s when Charles V assumed the imperial throne. The political dangers associated with religious reform were too dangerous, given the spread of Luther's movement. The Inquisition now focused its attention on these reform movements, and Converso intellectuals opted for other means of conveying their dissent.[100]

As time passed, the majority of the 16th century Conversos in Spain may not have been active Judaizers, but as Kevin Ingram notes, to assume that they assimilated is also ill-advised. Conversos saw themselves as distinct if not superior to their Old Christian neighbors. While their knowledge of Judaism may have declined, their sense of higher status and distinction because of their Jewish background remained. The

---

[100] Ibid., 5.

Conversos were the heirs of G-d's chosen people and not the descendants of "idol worshippers" like their Old Christian neighbors. [101] Many Conversos escaped to openly practicing Jewish communities from the 15th to the 17th centuries or created their own communities. Their struggles and successes drew other Conversos to join them in their recapturing of Jewish identity.

---

[101] Ibid., 8.

Glossary of Frequently Used Terms

Arabic (Ar); Hebrew (Heb); Spanish (Sp)

Agunah (Heb**) – A** previously married woman unable to remarry due to the lack of a Jewish divorce document.

Aljama (Ar**)** - A term used in official documents in Iberian kingdoms to label the self-governing communities of Moors and Jews living under Christian rule in the Iberian Peninsula.

Alcalde Mayor (Sp**)** - A local, administrative, and judicial official.

Alguacil (Sp**)** - A Spanish term referring a judge or the governor of a town or fortress. The aguacils of higher importance were referred to as Aguaciles Mayores.

Anusim (Heb**)** - A term referring to forced converts. It is a category of Jews in Jewish law who were converted forcibly to another religion.

Beit Din (Heb**)** - A Jewish court of law. A Beit Din traditionally consists of three observant Jewish men, capable of deciding Jewish legal matters.

Cohen (Heb**)** - A Hebrew term referring to a Jew descended from the Aaronic priesthood.

Converso (Sp**)** - A Jew or Muslim, who converted to Catholicism in Spain or Portugal during the 14th and 15th centuries, or one of their descendants.

Convivencia (Sp**)** - The period of Spanish history from the Muslim Umayyad conquest of Hispania in the early eighth century and which continued for several hundred years. It typically connotes peaceful coexistence between Muslims, Christians, and Jews.

Corregidor (Sp) - A local, administrative and judicial official in Spain.

Cortes (Sp) - A Spanish parliament in which prelates, nobles, and commoners participated.

Dhimmis (Ar) - The name applied by the Muslim conquerors to indigenous non-Muslim populations (i.e. Christians, Jews, etc.) who surrendered to Muslim control.

Geonim (Heb) - The heads of the two great Babylonian, Talmudic Academies of Sura and Pumbedita.

Get (Heb) - A Jewish divorce document.

Haliza (Heb) - The procedure for the *yavam* to forgo marriage and release the widow to remarry whomever she wished.

Hildago (Sp) - A member of the Spanish or Portuguese nobility.

Iggeret Hashamad (Heb) - The Epistle Concerning Apostasy written by Moses ben Maimon in which he discusses what constitutes sanctification or desecration of G-d's Name and the acceptance of forcibly converted Jews to Islam

Infante (Sp) - A Spanish title given to the sons and daughters (infantas) of the king in the various Christian Iberian kingdoms.

Karaites- A Jewish movement characterized by the recognition of the Hebrew Scriptures as its sole supreme legal authority as opposed to rabbinic Judaism, which considers the Oral Torah, to provide authoritative interpretations of the Torah.

Karet (Heb) - Spiritual excision from the Jewish people.

Kashrut (Heb**)** - Jewish religious dietary laws derived from the Written and Oral Laws.

Ketubah (Heb**)** - A Jewish wedding contract.

Las Siete Partidas (Sp**)** - A Castilian law code compiled during the reign of King Alfonso X of Castile (1252–1284). It was intended to establish a uniform body of legislation for the kingdom.

Limpieza de Sangre (Sp**)** – A phrase meaning "purity of blood." It referred to those who were regarded as pure "Old Christians," without Muslim or Jewish ancestors.

Levirate Marriage - A case in which the husband had died and his wife remained childless, and the brother in law was to marry the widow by biblical law.

Levir/Yavam (Heb**)** - The brother in law, bound to perform a levirate marriage.

Mahamad (Heb**)** – The governing board of each Spanish and Portuguese Jewish communities established in Western European cities.

Marrano (Spanish**)** - A derogatory term meaning swine or pig. It was often used to designate Conversos who Judaized.

Matzah (Heb) – Unleavened bread eaten during Passover.

Mikveh (Heb**)** - A ritual bath used for the purpose of ritual immersion in Judaism.

Mishnah (Heb**)** - The first major written redaction of Jewish oral traditions known as the Oral Torah. Together with the Gemara, it forms the Talmud.

Mitzvot (Heb) - The commandments of the Written and Oral Law.

Mohel (Heb) – A Jewish person trained to perform circumcision.

New Christian – Another term used for Conversos to distinguish them from Old Christians. Old Christians were Christians prior to 1391 and did not have Jewish or Muslim heritage. The term was often used in Portugal. For the sake of simplicity, the term Converso is used throughout this work.

Niddah (Heb) - A term which refers to a woman during her menstrual cycle. It also relates to a woman who has menstruated and not completed the requirement of immersion in a mikveh (ritual bath) before resuming marital relations with her husband.

Noahides- Refers to non-Jews observing the Seven Noahide Laws which include moral and ethical aspects.

Oral Law - Rabbinic Judaism maintains that the Torah was revealed in Written and Oral form. The written text is comprised of the "Books of Moses," The Oral Torah provides the interpretation and implementation of the commandments outlined in the Written Torah.

Shulchan Aruch (Heb) - literally the "Set table"; the principal code of Jewish law written in the 16th century.

Talmud (Heb) - A central text of Rabbinic Judaism composed of the Mishnah and its commentary, the Gemara.

Talit (Heb) - A Jewish prayer shawl. The tallit is donned during the morning prayers or all the services of Yom Kippur.

Tefillin (Heb) - Small black leather boxes containing scrolls of parchment. The scrolls inscribed with verses from the Torah. They are worn by religious Jews during weekday morning prayers.

Terumah (Heb) - A food item given to a priest, as a gift.

Tosefta (Heb) - A compilation of the Jewish oral law from the late 2nd-century period, the period of the Mishnah.

Tosafot (Heb) - Medieval commentaries on the Talmud.

Tzitzit (Heb) – Ritual fringes worn on a four cornered garment or on a Tallit in accordance with Numbers 15:37-40.

Zohar (Heb) - The principle book of Jewish mysticism.

Bibliography

Abrera, Anna Ysabel D. *The Tribunal of Zaragoza and Crypto-Judaism, 1484-1515*. Turnhout, Belgium: Brepols, 2008.

Adler, Cyrus, and Isidore Singer. "Inquisition." Jewish Encyclopedia. 1906. Accessed June 9, 2015. http://www.jewishencyclopedia.com/articles/8122-inquisition.

Adler, Cyrus, and Isidore Singer. "Apostasy and Apostates from Judaism." Jewish Encyclopedia. 1906. Accessed June 9, 2015. http://www.jewishencyclopedia.com/articles/1654-apostasy-and-apostates-from-judaism.

"Al-Taqiyya, Dissimulation Part 1." Al Islam. Accessed June 2, 2015. http://www.al-islam.org/shiite-encyclopedia-ahlul-bayt-dilp-team/al-taqiyya-dissimulation-part-1.

Albert, Bat-Sheva. "Isidore of Seville: His Attitude Towards Judaism and His Impact on Early Medieval Canon Law." *The Jewish Quarterly Review* 80, no. 3-4 (1990): 207-20.

Alfassa, Shelomo. *The Sephardic 'Anousim': The Forcibly Converted Jews of Spain and Portugal*. New York: ISLC, 2010.

Alpert, Michael. *Crypto-judaism and the Spanish Inquisition*. Basingstoke, Hampshire: Palgrave, 2001.

Alter, Alexandra. "'Secret Jews' of the Spanish Inquisition." Derkeiler. August 6, 2005. Accessed March 30, 2015. http://newsgroups.derkeiler.com/Archive/Soc/soc.culture.cuba/2005-08/msg00977.html.

Altmann, Alexander. "Eternality of Punishment: A Theological Controversy within the Amsterdam Rabbinate in the Thirties of the Seventeenth Century." *Proceedings of the American Academy for Jewish Research* 40 (1972): 1-88.

Amital, Yehuda. "A Torah Perspective on the Status of Secular Jews Today." The Israel Koschitzky Virtual Beit Midrash. Accessed January 13, 2015. http://etzion.org.il/vbm/english/alei/2-2chilo.htm.

Amran, Rica. "Judíos Y Conversos En Las Crónicas De Los Reyes De Castilla (desde Finales Del Siglo XIV Hasta La Expulsión)." *Espacio, Tiempo Y Forma* Serie III, no. 9 (1996): 257-76.

Antine, Nissan. "Responsa Relating to the Conversos." Lecture, from Beth Sholom and Talmud Torah, Potomac, January 1, 2010.

Antonio Escudero, José. "Luis Vives Y La Inquisicion." *Revista De La Inquisición : Intolerancia Y Derechos Humanos* 13 (2009): 11-24.

Assis, Yom Tov. "The Jews of the Maghreb and Sepharad: A Case Study of Inter-communal Cultural Relations through the Ages." *El Prezente* 2 (2008): 11-30.

Baer, Yitzhak. *A History of the Jews in Christian Spain.* Vol. II. Philadelphia: Jewish Publication Society of America, 1961.

Barnai, Jacob. "Christian Messianism and the Portuguese Marranos: The Emergence of Sabbateanism in Smyrna." *Jew History Jewish History* 7, no. 2 (1993): 119-26.

Baron, Salo W. *A Social and Religious History of the Jews.* Vol. IV. Philadelphia: Jewish Publication Society, 1957.

Baron, Salo W. *A Social and Religious History of the Jews.* Vol. IX. New York: Columbia University Press, 1965.

Baron, Salo W. *A Social and Religious History of the Jews.* Vol. X. Philadelphia: Jewish Publication Society, 1965.

Baron, Salo W. *A Social and Religious History of the Jews.* Vol. XI. Philadelphia: Jewish Publication Society, 1967.

Baron, Salo W. *A Social and Religious History of the Jews.* Vol. XIII. Philadelphia: Jewish Publication Society, 1969.

Baxter Wolf, Kenneth. "Sentencia-Estatuto De Toledo, 1449." Texts in Translation. 2008. Accessed June 2, 2015. https://sites.google.com/site/canilup/toledo1449.

Beinart, Haim, and Yael Guiladi. *Conversos on Trial: The Inquisition in Ciudad Real.* Jerusalem: Magnes Press, Hebrew University, 1981.

Beinart, Haim. *The Expulsion of the Jews from Spain.* Oxford: Littman Library of Jewish Civilization, 2002.

Ben-Sasson, Menahem. "On the Jewish Identity of Forced
    Converts: A Study of Forced Conversion in the Almohade
    Period." *Pe'amim* 42 (1990): 16-37.
Ben-Shalom, Ram. "Between Official and Private Dispute: The
    Case of Christian Spain and Provence in the Late Middle
    Ages." *AJS Review* 27, no. 1, 23-71.
Ben-Shalom, Ram. "The Converso as Subversive: Jewish
    Traditions or Christian Libel?" *Journal of Jewish Studies* 50,
    no. 2 (1999): 259-83.
Ben-Shalom, Ram. "The Typology of the Converso in Isaac
    Abravanel's Biblical Exegesis." *Jew History Jewish History* 23,
    no. 3 (2009): 281-92.
Ben-Ur, Aviva. ""Fakelore" or Historically Overlooked Sub-
    Ethnic Group?" HNet Humanities and Social Sciences
    Online. 2010. Accessed June 9, 2015. http://www.h-
    net.org/reviews/showrev.php?id=29438.
Benveniste, Arthur. "Finding Our Lost Brothers and Sisters: The
    Crypto Jews of Brazil." *Western States Jewish History* 29, no.
    3 (1997): 103-09.
Benveniste, Henriette-Rika. "On the Language of Conversion:
    Visigothic Spain Revisited." *Historein* 6 (2006): 72-87.
Berenbaum, Michael, and Fred Skolnik eds. "Isaac Ben Sheshet
    Perfet." *Encyclopedia Judaica*. 2nd ed. Vol. 10. Detroit:
    Macmillan, 2007.
Bermúdez Vázquez, Manuel. "Intuiciones De Criptojudaísmo En
    El "Quod Nihil Scitur" De Francisco Sánchez." *Revista
    Internacional De Filosofía* 13 (2008): 285-94.
Bermúdez Vázquez, Manuel. "La Influencia Del Pensamiento
    Judeo-cristiano En Michel De Montaigne, Giordano
    Bruno Y Francisco Sánchez." *Ámbitos* 23 (2010): 19-27.
Bodian, Miriam. "Hebrews of the Portuguese Nation: The
    Ambiguous Boundaries of Self-Definition." *Jewish Social
    Studies* 15, no. 1 (2008): 66-80.
Bodian, Miriam. *Hebrews of the Portuguese Nation: Conversos and
    Community in Early Modern Amsterdam*. Bloomington:
    Indiana University Press, 1997.

"B'nei Anusim." Be'chol Lashon. Accessed June 9, 2015. http://www.bechollashon.org/projects/spanish/anusim.php.

Carpenter, Dwayne. "From Al-Burak to Alboraycos: The Art of Transformation on the Eve of the Expulsion." In *Jews and Conversos at the Time of the Expulsion.* Jerusalem: Zalman Shazar for Jewish History, 1999.

Carvajal, Luis De, and Seymour B. Liebman. *The Enlightened; the Writings of Luis De Carvajal, El Mozo.* Coral Gables, Fla.: University of Miami Press, 1967.

Carvalho, Joaquim. *Religion and Power in Europe: Conflict and Convergence.* Pisa: PLUS-Pisa University Press, 2007.

Chazan, Robert. *European Jewry and the First Crusade.* Berkeley: University of California Press, 1987.

Cohen, Jeremy. "Between Martyrdom and Apostasy: Doubt and Self-definition in Twelfth-century Ashkenaz." *Journal of Medieval and Early Modern Studies* 29, no. 3 (1999): 431-71.

Cohen, Mark R. *Under Crescent and Cross: The Jews in the Middle Ages.* Princeton, N.J.: Princeton University Press, 1994.

Cohen, Shaye J. D. *The Beginnings of Jewishness Boundaries, Varieties, Uncertainties.* Berkeley: University of California Press, 1999.

"Conversos & Crypto-Jews." City of Albuquerque. Accessed June 9, 2015. http://www.cabq.gov/humanrights/public-information-and-education/diversity-booklets/jewish-american-heritage/conversos-crypto-jews.

"Crypto Jews." Am I Jewish? Accessed March 25, 2015. http://www.amijewish.info/w/crypto-jews/.

Cutler, Allan Harris, and Helen Elmquist Cutler. *The Jew as Ally of the Muslim: Medieval Roots of Anti-Semitism.* Notre Dame, Ind.: University of Notre Dame Press, 1986.

Davidson, Herbert A. *Moses Maimonides: The Man and His Works.* Oxford: Oxford University Press, 2005.

Dorff, Elliot N., and Arthur I. Rosett. *A Living Tree the Roots and Growth of Jewish Law.* Albany, N.Y.: the State University of New York Press, 1988.

Faur, Jose. *In the Shadow of History Jews and Conversos at the Dawn of Modernity.* Albany, N.Y.: the State University of New York Press, 1992.

Faur, José. "Four Classes of Conversos." *Revue Des Études Juives* 149, no. 1-2 (1990): 113-24.

Faur, José. "Anti-Maimonidean Demons." *Review of Rabbinic Judaism* 6 (2003): 3-52.

Ferry, Barbara, and Debbie Nathan. "Mistaken Identity? The Case of New Mexico's "Hidden Jews." The Atlantic. December 1, 2000. Accessed April 1, 2015. http://www.theatlantic.com/magazine/archive/2000/12 /mistaken-identity-the-case-of-new-mexicos-hidden-jews/378454/ I.

Ferziger, Adam S. "Between 'Ashkenazi' and Sepharad: An Early Modern German Rabbinic Response to Religious Pluralism in the Spanish-Portuguese Community." *Studia Rosenthaliana* 35, no. 1 (2001): 7-22.

Fishman, Talya. "The Jewishness of the Conversos." Lecture, Early Modern Workshop: Jewish History Resources, January 1, 2004.

Foer, Paul, and Chananette Pascal Cohen. "For Hispanic 'Crypto-Jews,' Lawsuits May Follow Religious Rediscovery." JNS. October 29, 2012. Accessed March 25, 2015. http://www.jns.org/latest-articles/2012/10/29/for-hispanic-crypto-jews-lawsuits-may-follow-religious-redis.html#.VXdW0dLBzGd.

Fram, Edward. "Perception and Reception of Repentant Apostates in Medieval Ashkenaz and Premodern Poland." *AJS Review* 21, no. 2 (1996): 299-339.

Frank, Daniel, and Matt Goldfish. *Rabbinic Culture and Its Critics: Jewish Authority, Dissent, and Heresy in the Medieval and Early Modern Times.* Detroit: Wayne State University, 2007.

Friedenwald, Harry. "Montaigne's Relation to Judaism and the Jews." *The Jewish Quarterly Review* 31, no. 2 (1940): 141-48.

Furst, Rachel. "Captivity, Conversion, and Communal Identity: Sexual Angst and Religious Crisis in Frankfurt, 1241." *Jew History Jewish History* 22, no. 1-2 (2008): 179-221.

Gampel, Benjamin R. "The 'Identity' of Sephardim of Medieval Christian Iberia." *Jewish Social Studies* 8, no. 2/3 (2002): 133-38.

Gerber, Jane S. *The Jews of Spain.* New York: The Free Press, 1992.

Gilman, Stephen. *The Spain of Fernando De Rojas; the Intellectual and Social Landscape of La Celestina.* Princeton, N.J.: Princeton University Press, 1972.

Gitlitz, David M. *Secrecy and Deceit: The Religion of the Crypto-Jews.* Philadelphia: Jewish Publication Society, 1996.

Goldish, Matt. *The Sabbatean Prophets.* Cambridge, Mass.: Harvard University Press, 2004.

Golinkin, David. "How Can Apostates Such as the Falash Mura Return to Judaism?" *Responsa in a Moment* 1, no. 5 (2007). Accessed June 9, 2015. http://www.schechter.edu/responsa.aspx?ID=30.

Gomez-Hortiguela Amillo, Angel. "La Vida Sine Querella De Juan Luis Vives." *EHumanista* 26 (2014): 345-56.

Grayzel, Solomon. "The Beginnings of Exclusion." *The Jewish Quarterly Review* 61, no. 1 (1970): 15-26.

Grayzel, Solomon. *The Church and the Jews in the XIIIth Century.* New York: Hermon, 1966.

Green, Simcha. "Welcoming Anusim Back Into The Family." The Jewish Press. August 22, 2012. Accessed March 25, 2015. http://www.jewishpress.com/indepth/opinions/welcoming-anusim-back-into-the-family/2010/12/08/0/?print.

Green, Toby. *The Reign of Fear.* London: Macmillan: 2007.

Guerson, Alexandra. "Seeking Remission: Jewish Conversion in the Crown of Aragon, C.1378–1391." *Jewish History* 24, no. 1 (2010): 33-52.

Gutwirth, Eleazar. "The Jews in 15th Century Castilian Chronicles." *The Jewish Quarterly Review* 74, no. 4 (1984): 379-96.

Halevy, Schulamith C., and Nachum Dershowitz. "Obscure Practices among New World Anusim." *Proceedings of the Conferencia Internacional De Investigacion De La Asociacion Latinoamericana De Estudios Judaicos,* 1995. Accessed June 9, 2015.

Haliczer, Stephen. "Conversos Y Judíos En Tiempos De La Expulsión : Un Análisis Crítico De Investigación Y Análisis." *Revistas Espacio, Tiempo Y Forma* Serie III (1993): 287-300.

"Jewish History Sourcebook: The Jews of Spain and the Visigothic Code, 654-681 CE." Fordham University. 1998. Accessed June 2, 2015. http://legacy.fordham.edu/halsall/jewish/jews-visigothic1.asp.

Halperin, David J. trans. Abraham Miguel Cardozo; Selected Writings. New York: Paulist Press, 2001.

Hayim Sofer, Yitshaq BenTsvi Ben Naftali. *Sefer Shu "T Ha-Radbaz Mi-Ktav Yad*. Benei Brak, 1975.

Hershman, A.M. *Rabbi Isaac Bar Sheshet Perfet and His Times*. New York, N.Y.: Jewish Theological Seminary, 1943.

Hinojosa Montalvo, José. "Los Judios En La España Medieval: De La Tolerancia a La Expulsión." In *Los Marginados En El Mundo Medieval Y Moderno.*, 25-41. Almería: Instituto De Estudios Almerienses, 1998.

Hochbaum, Jerry. "Who Is a Jew: A Sociological Perspective." *Tradition* 13/14, no. 4/1 (1973): 35-41.

Hopstein, Avner. "The Crypto-Jews of Brazil." Y Net News. October 26, 2006. Accessed March 31, 2015. http://www.ynetnews.com/articles/0,7340,L-3319972,00.html.

Hordes, Stanley M. *To the End of the Earth: A History of the Crypto-Jews of New Mexico*. New York: Columbia University Press, 2005.

Idel, Moshe. *Messianic Mystics*. New Haven: Yale University Press, 1998.

Ingram, Kevin. *Secret Lives, Public Lies the Conversos and Socio-religious Non-conformism in the Spanish Golden Age*. San Diego, California: UC San Diego Electronic Theses and Dissertations, 2006.

Ingram, Kevin, ed. *The Conversos and Moriscos in Late Medieval Spain and beyond*. Vol. 2. Leiden: Brill, 2012.

Israel, Jonathan. "Sephardic Immigration into the Dutch Republic, 1595-1672." *Studia Rosenthaliana* 23 (1989): 45-53.

Israel, Jonathan. "Spain and the Dutch Sephardim, 1609-1660." *Studia Rosenthaliana* 12, no. 1/2 (1978): 1-61.

Jacobs, Louis. "Attitudes towards Christianity in the Halakhah." Louis Jacobs. 2005. Accessed June 1, 2015.

http://louisjacobs.org/articles/attitudes-towards-christianity-in-the-halakhah/?highlight=Attitudes towards Christianity.

Jocz, Jakob. *The Jewish People and Jesus Christ; a Study in the Relationship between the Jewish People and Jesus Christ.* London: S.P.C.K., 1949.

JOSPIC -J Staff "A List of 134 Books Containing Marrano, Converso, Crypto Jew, Secret Jew, Hidden Jew, New Christian, or Anusim in the Title or Subtitle: Changes in Usage Over 86 Years." *Journal of Spanish, Portuguese, and Italian Crypto-Jews*, 2011, 149-55.

Juster, J. *Les Juifs Dans L'Empire Romain.* Vol. II. Paris: P. Geunther, 1914.

Kaplan, Yosef. "The Portuguese Jews in Amsterdam: From Forced Conversion to a Return to Judaism." *Studia Rosenthaliana* 15, no. 1 (1981): 37-51.

Kaplan, Yosef. "The Jewish Profile of the Spanish-Portuguese Community of London during the Seventeenth Century." *Judaism* 41, no. 3 (1992): 229-40.

Kaplan, Yosef. "Wayward New Christians and Stubborn New Jews: The Shaping of a Jewish Identity." *Jewish History* 8, no. 1-2 (1994): 27-41.

Katz, Jacob. *Exclusiveness and Tolerance; Studies in Jewish-gentile Relations in Medieval and Modern Times.* West Orange: Behrman House, 1961.

Katz, Jacob. *Halakhah Ve-Qabbalah.* Jerusalem: Magnes Press, 1984.

Katz, Solomon. *The Jews in the Visigothic and Frankish Kingdoms of Spain and Gaul.* New York: Kraus, 1970.

Kedourie, Elie. *Spain and the Jews: The Sephardi Experience: 1492 and after.* London: Thames and Hudson, 1992.

Kelly, David. "DNA Clears the Fog Over Latino Links to Judaism in New Mexico." Los Angeles Times. December 5, 2004. Accessed March 25, 2015. http://articles.latimes.com/2004/dec/05/nation/na-heritage5.

Krow-Lucal, Martha G. "Marginalizing History: Observations on the Origins of the Inquisition in Fifteenth-century Spain by B. Netanyahu." *Judaism*, 1997, 47-62.

Kunin, David A. "Welcoming Back the Anusim: A Halakhic Teshuvah." Sephardim Hope. July 9, 2009. Accessed June 10, 2015. http://sephardimhope.net/index.php?view=article&catid=36:articles&id=62:welcoming-back-the-anusim-a-halakhic-teshuvah&format=pdf&option=com_content&Itemid=69.

Lavender, Abraham D. "The Secret Jews (Neofiti) of Sicily: Religious and Social Status Before and After the Inquisition." *Journal of Spanish, Portuguese, and Italian Crypto-Jews* 3 (2011): 119-33.

Lawrance, Jeremy. "Alegoría Y Apocalipsis En "El Alboraique"" *Revista De Poética Medieval* 11 (2003): 11-39.

Lazar, Moshe. *The Jews of Spain and the Expulsion of 1492*. Lancaster, Calif.: Labyrinthos, 1997.

Lea, Henry Charles. "Ferrand Martinez and the Massacres of 1391." *The American Historical Review* 1, no. 2 (1896): 209-19.

Leibman, Seymour. *The Jews in New Spain*. Miami: University of Miami, 1970.

Lent, Dani. "Analysis of the Israeli High Courts: Jewish Apostates and the Law of Return." Kol Hamevaser. 2010. Accessed June 1, 2015. http://www.kolhamevaser.com/2010/09/analysis-of-the-israeli-high-court-jewish-apostates-and-the-law-of-return/.

Lewis, Bernard. *The Jews of Islam*. Princeton, N.J.: Princeton University Press, 1984.

Lichenstein, Aharon. *Brother Daniel and Jewish Fraternity, Leaves of Faith: The World of Jewish Living*. Jersey City: Ktav, 2004.

Lieberman, Julia R. "Sermons and the Construct of a Jewish Identity: The Hamburg Sephardic Community in the 1620s." *Jewish Studies Quarterly* 10, no. 1 (2003): 49-72.

Liebman, Seymour B. *The Jews in New Spain; Faith, Flame, and the Inquisition,* Coral Gables, Fla.: University of Miami Press, 1970.

Liebman, Seymour B. *New World Jewry, 1493-1825: Requiem for the Forgotten.* New York: Ktav Pub. House, 1982.

Linder, Amnon. *The Jews in Roman Imperial Legislation.* Detroit, Mich.: Wayne State University Press, 1987.

Lindo, E.H. *The Jews of Spain and Portugal.* London: Longman, Brown, Green, & Longmans, 1848.

Lipshiz, Cnaan. "Secret No More." Shavei Israel. November 9, 2009. Accessed March 25, 2015. http://www.shavei.org/communities/bnei_anousim/artic les-bnei_anousim/secret-no-more/?lang=en.

Llobet Portella, Josep Maria. "Los Conversos Según La Documentación Local De Cervera (1338-1501)." *Revista De La Facultad De Geografía E Historia* 4 (1989): 335-49.

Maimonides, Moses, and Abraham S. Halkin. *Crisis and Leadership: Epistles of Maimonides.* Philadelphia: Jewish Publication Society of America, 1985.

Marcus, Jacob Rader. *The Jew in the Medieval World: A Source Book, 315-1791.* Cincinnati: Union of American Hebrew Congregations, 1938.

Margaliot, Reuben. *Sefer Ḥasidim.* Jerusalem: Mosad Ha-Rav Ḳooḳ, 1956.

"Marranos, Conversos & New Christians." Jewish Virtual Library. Accessed June 1, 2015. https://www.jewishvirtuallibrary.org/jsource/Judaism/M arranos.html.

Martin, J. J. "Marranos and Nicodemites in Sixteenth-Century Venice." *Journal of Medieval and Early Modern Studies* 41, no. 3 (2011): 577-99.

Mentzer, Raymond A. "Marranos of Southern France in the Early Sixteenth Century." *The Jewish Quarterly Review* 72, no. 4 (1982): 303-11.

Metzger, David, ed. *Sheelot U-Teshuvot Le-rabbenu Ha-gadol Marana Ve-rabbana Ha-rav Yiẓḥaḳ Bar Sheshet.* Jerusalem: Makhon Or HaMizrah, 1993.

Meyers, Charles, and Norman Simms eds. *Troubled Souls: Conversos, Crypto-Jews, and Other Confused Jewish Intellectuals from the Fourteenth through the Eighteenth Century.* Hamilton: Outrigger Publishers, 2001.

Meyerson, Mark D. "Aragonese and Catalan Jewish Converts at the Time of the Expulsion." *Jewish History*, 1992, 131-49.

Meyerson, Mark D. *A Jewish Renaissance in Fifteenth-century Spain.* Princeton: Princeton University Press, 2004.

Montalvo, Jose. *The Jews of the Kingdom of Valencia: From Persecution to Expulsion, 1391-1492.* Jerusalem: Magnes Press, Hebrew University, 1993.

Nelson, Zalman. "Is a Jew Who Converts Still Jewish?" Chabad. Accessed June 2, 2015. http://www.chabad.org/library/article_cdo/aid/1269075 /jewish/Is-a-Jew-Who-Converts-Still-Jewish.htm.

Netanyahu, B. "Americo Castro and His View of the Origins of the Pureza De Sangre." *Proceedings of the American Academy for Jewish Research* 46/47, no. Jubilee Volume (1928-29 / 1978-79) (1979): 397-457.

Netanyahu, B. *The Origins of the Inquisition in Fifteenth Century Spain.* New York: Random House, 1995.

Netanyahu, B. *The Marranos of Spain: From the Late 14th to the Early 16th Century, According to Contemporary Hebrew Sources.* 3rd ed. Ithaca, N.Y.: Cornell University Press, 1999.

Nirenberg, David. "Conversion, Sex, And Segregation: Jews And Christians In Medieval Spain." *The American Historical Review* 107, no. 4 (2002): 1065-093.

Nirenberg, David. *Anti-Judaism: The Western Tradition.* New York: W. W. Norton &, 2013.

Nissimi, Hilda. "Religious Conversion, Covert Defiance and Social Identity: A Comparative View." *Numen* 51, no. 4 (2004): 367-406.

"Obituary Samuel Lerer, an American Rabbi Who Converted Mexicans, Dies at 89." Jewish Telegraph Agency. February 9, 2004. Accessed March 25, 2015. http://www.jta.org/2004/02/09/archive/obituary-samuel-lerer-an-american-rabbi-who-converted-mexicans-dies-at-89.

Oeltjen, Natalie. *Crisis and Regeneration: The Conversos of Majorca, 1391-1416.* Toronto: University of Toronto, 2012.

Orme, Wyatt. "Crypto-Jews' In the Southwest Find Faith in a Shrouded Legacy." Code Switch Frontiers of Race, Culture, and Ethnicity. February 19, 2014. Accessed March 25, 2015. http://www.npr.org/sections/codeswitch/2014/02/19/275862633/crypto-jews-in-the-southwest-find-faith-in-a-shrouded-legacy.

Parello, Vincent. "La Apologética Antijudía De Juan Luis Vives (1543)." *Melanges De La Casa De Velazquez* 38, no. 2 (2008): 171-87.

Perez, Joseph, and Lysa Hochroth. *History of a Tragedy: The Expulsion of the Jews from Spain.* Chicago: University of Illinois Press, 1993.

Perlmann, Moshe. "Apostasy." Jewish Virtual Library. 2008. Accessed June 2, 2015. http://www.jewishvirtuallibrary.org/jsource/judaica/ejud_0002_0002_0_01188.html.

Popkin, Richard H. *The History of Scepticism from Erasmus to Spinoza.* Rev. and Expanded ed. Berkeley: University of California Press, 1979.

"Portugal." Jewish Virtual Library, accessed on July 28, 2015, http://www.jewishvirtuallibrary.org/jsource/vjw/Portugal.html

Quesada Morillas, Yolanda. "La Expulsion De Los Judios Andaluces a Finales Del Siglo XV Y Su Prohibicion De Pase a Indias." *Actas Del I Congreso Internacional Sobre Migraciones En Andalucia*, 2011, 2099-106.

Rábade Obrado, María Del Pilar. "La Instrucción Cristiana De Los Conversos En La Castilla Del Siglo XV." *En La España Medieval* 22 (1999): 369-93.

Raphael, Amia. "Goldsmiths and Silversmiths." Jewish Virtual Library, accessed on July 31, 2015. http://www.jewishvirtuallibrary.org/jsource/judaica/ejud_0002_0007_0_07579.html.

Rosenblatt, Eli. "Picturing Today's Conversos." The Forward. April 1, 2008. Accessed March 25, 2015.

http://forward.com/culture/13079/picturing-today-s-conversos-01595/.

Rosenbloom, Noah H. "Menasseh Ben Israel and the Eternality of Punishment Issue." *Proceedings of the American Academy for Jewish Research* 60 (1994): 241-62.

Rosenstock, Bruce. "Abraham Miguel Cardoso's Messianism: A Reappraisal." *AJS Review* 23, no. 1 (1998): 63-104.

Ross, Theodore. "Shalom on the Range: In Search of the American Crypto-Jew." Harpers. December 1, 2009. Accessed March 27, 2015. http://harpers.org/archive/2009/12/shalom-on-the-range/.

Roth, Cecil. *A History of the Marranos.* Philadelphia: Jewish Publication Society of America, 1947.

Roth, Cecil. *The Spanish Inquisition.* New York: WW. Norton and Company, 1964.

Roth, Norman. "Anti-Converso Riots of the Fifteenth Century, Pulgar, and the Inquisition." *En La España Medieval* 15 (1992): 367-94.

Roth, Norman. *Jews, Visigoths, and Muslims in Medieval Spain: Cooperation and Conflict.* Leiden: E.J. Brill, 1994.

Roth, Norman. *Conversos, Inquisition, and the Expulsion of the Jews from Spain.* Madison, Wis.: University of Wisconsin Press, 1995.

Ruderman, David B. *Jewish Thought and Scientific Discovery in Early Modern Europe.* Detroit, Michigan: Wayne State University, 2001.

Sachar, Howard Morley. *Farewell España: The World of the Sephardim Remembered.* New York: Knopf, 1995.

Salomon, H.P. "New Light on the Portuguese Inquisition: The Second Reply to the Archbishop of Cranganor." *Studia Rosenthaliana* 5, no. 2 (1971): 178-86.

Sanchez, Francisco, and Douglas F.S. Thomson. *That Nothing Is Known.* Edited by Elaine Limbrick. Cambridge: Cambridge University Press, 1988.

Saperstein, Marc. "Christianity, Christians, and 'New Christians' in the Sermons of Saul Levi Morteira." *Hebrew Union College Annual* 70/71:329-84.

Saperstein, Marc. "Saul Levi Morteira's Treatise on the Immortality of the Soul." *Studia Rosenthaliana* 25, no. 2 (1991): 131-48.

Schiffman, Lawrence H. *Who Was a Jew?: Rabbinic and Halakhic Perspectives on the Jewish-Christian Schism*. Hoboken, N.J.: Ktav Pub. House, 1985.

Scholberg, Kenneth R. "Minorities in Medieval Castilian Literature." *Hispania* 37, no. 2 (1954): 203-09.

Scholem, Gershom. *The Messianic Idea in Judaism: And Other Essays on Jewish Spirituality*. New York: Schocken Books, 1972.

Selke, Angela. *Los Chuetas Y La Inquisicion*. Madrid: Taurus, 1972.

Shatzmiller, Joseph. "Converts and Judaizers in the Early Fourteenth Century." *Harvard Theological Review* 74, no. 1 (1981): 63-77.

Sherwin, Byron L. *Faith Finding Meaning: A Theology of Judaism*. Oxford: Oxford University Press, 2009.

Singer, Isidore, and Cyrus Adler, eds. "Spain." *Jewish Encylopedia*. 1906.

Spinoza, Benedictus De, and Dagobert D. Runes. *The Ethics Of Spinoza: The Road to Inner Freedom*. Secaucus: Citadel, 1976.

Stern, Sacha. *Jewish Identity in Early Rabbinic Writings*. New York: Brill, 1994.

Stillman, Norman A. *The Jews of Arab Lands: A History and Source Book*. Philadelphia: Jewish Publication Society of America, 1979.

Suarez Bilbao, Fernando. "Cristianos Contra Judios y Conversos." Lecture, from Universidad Rey Juan Carlos, Madrid, January 1, 2004.

Swetschinski, Daniel M. "Kinship and Commerce: The Foundations of Portuguese Jewish Life in Seventeenth-Century Holland." *Studia Rosenthaliana* 15, no. 1 (1981): 52-74.

Synan, Edward A. *The Popes and the Jews in the Middle Ages*. New York: Macmillan, 1965.

Szajkowski, Zosa. "Trade Relations of Marranos in France with the Iberian Peninsula in the Sixteenth and Seventeenth Centuries." *The Jewish Quarterly Review* 50, no. 1 (1959): 69-78.

Thornton, Stuart. "Hidden History: Rabbi Explains the Identity of the Crypto-Jews." National Geographic. Accessed March 25, 2015. http://www.nationalgeographic.com/hidden-history/.

Touger, Eliyahu. "Avodah Kochavim - Chapter Two." Chabad. Accessed June 9, 2015. http://www.chabad.org/library/article_cdo/aid/912360/jewish/Avodah-Kochavim-Chapter-Two.htm.

Touger, Eliyahu. "Ma'achalot Assurot - Chapter 17." Chabad. Accessed June 9, 2015. http://www.chabad.org/library/article_cdo/aid/968273/jewish/Maachalot-Assurot-Chapter-17.htm.

Touger, Eliyahu. "Gerushin - Chapter Three." Chabad. Accessed June 9, 2015. http://www.chabad.org/library/article_cdo/aid/957708/jewish/Gerushin-Chapter-Three.htm.

Touger, Eliyahu. "Yibbum VChalitzah - Chapter One." Chabad. Accessed June 9, 2015. http://www.chabad.org/library/article_cdo/aid/960619/jewish/Yibbum-vChalitzah-Chapter-One.htm.

Treatman, Ronit. "Queen Esther: Patron Saint of Crypto-Jews." The Times of Israel. March 16, 2014. Accessed April 2, 2015. http://www.timesofisrael.com/queen-esther-patron-saint-of-crypto-jews/.

Usque, Samuel, and Martin Cohen. *Consolations for the Tribulations of Israel (Consolacam as Tribulacoens De Israel)*. Philadelphia: Jewish Publication Society of America, 1977.

Utterback, Kristine T. "'Conversi' Revert: Voluntary and Forced Return to Judaism in the Early Fourteenth Century." *Church History* 64, no. 1 (1995): 16-28.

Wakefield, Walter L. *Heresy, Crusade, and Inquisition in Southern France, 1100-1250*. Berkeley: University of California Press, 1974.

Wheelwright, Jeff. "The 'Secret Jews' of San Luis Valley." Smithsonian Magazine. 2008. Accessed March 25, 2015. http://www.smithsonianmag.com/science-nature/the-secret-jews-of-san-luis-valley-11765512/?no-ist.

Wildman, Sarah. "Mallorca's Jews Get Their Due: Spanish Island's Community Alive and Thriving." The Forward. April 13, 2012. Accessed March 27, 2015. http://forward.com/articles/154649/mallorcas-jews-get-their-due/?p=all#ixzz3TLpkmfSl.

Wiznitzer, Arnold. "Crypto-Jews in Mexico during the Sixteenth Century." *American Jewish Historical Quarterly* 51, no. 3 (1962): 168-214.

Yerushalmi, Yosef. "The Re-education of the Marranos in the Seventeenth Century." Scribd. 1980. Accessed June 2, 2015. http://www.scribd.com/doc/63071643/Re-Education-of-the-Marranos-by-Yosef-Yerushalmi#scribd.

Yerushalmi, Yosef Hayim. "The Inquisition and the Jews of France in the Time of Bernard Gui." *Harvard Theological Review* 63, no. 3 (1970): 317-76.

Yerushalmi, Yosef Hayim. *From Spanish Court to Italian Ghetto; Isaac Cardoso; a Study in Seventeenth-century Marranism and Jewish Apologetics.* New York: Columbia University Press, 1971.

Yovel, Yirmiyahu. "Converso Dualities In The First Generation: The Cancioneros." *Jewish Social Studies: History, Culture, and Society* 4, no. 3 (1998): 1-28.

Zeitlin, S. "Mumar and Meshumad." *The Jewish Quarterly Review* 54, no. 1 (1963): 84-86.

Zeldes, Nadia. "Legal Status of Jewish Converts to Christianity in Southern Italy and Provence." *California Italian Studies*, 1, no. 1 (2010). Accessed June 2, 2015. http://escholarship.org/uc/item/91z342hv.

Zohar, Zvi. "The Sephardic Tradition-Creative Responses to Modernity." Lecture, January 1, 2010.

Zsom, Dora. "Uncircumcised Converts in Sephardi Responsa from the Fifteenth and Sixteenth Centuries." *Iberoamerica Global* 1, no. 3 (2008): 159-71.

Zsom, Dora. "The Return of the Conversos to Judaism in the Ottoman Empire and North-Africa." *Hispania Judaica* 7 (2010): 335-47.

Zsom, Dora. "Converts in the Responsa of R. David Ibn Avi Zimra: An Analysis of the Texts." *Hispania Judaica* 6 (2008): 267-92.

Zsom, Dora. "The Levirate Marriage of Converts in the Responsa of Some Sephardic Authorities." *Kut* 3 (2008): 96-113.

De Covarrubias Horozco, Sebastian. "Tesoro De La Lengua Castellana O Española." Universidad De Sevilla-Fondo Antiguo. Accessed June 2, 2015. http://fondosdigitales.us.es/fondos/libros/765/1119/tesoro-de-la-lengua-castellana-o-espanola/.

De Salazar Acha, Jaime. "La Limpieza De Sangre." *Revista De La Inquisicion* 1 (1991): 289-308.

De Spinoza, Benedict, and R.H.M Elwes. *A Theologico-Political Treatise*. New York: Dover, 1951.

DeSola Cardoza, Anne. "Texas Mexican Secret Spanish Jews Today." Sefarad. Accessed June 9, 2015. http://sefarad.org/lm/011/texas.html.

Ldez, Andre, and Manuel Moreno. *Memorias Del Reinado De Los Reyes Católicos,*. Madrid: [Real Academia De La Historia], 1962.

ABOUT THE AUTHOR

Juan Marcos Bejarano Gutierrez is a graduate of the University of Texas at Dallas where he earned a bachelor of science in electrical engineering. He studied at the Siegal College of Judaic Studies and received a Master of Arts Degree in Judaic Studies. He completed his doctoral studies at the Spertus Institute in Chicago in 2015. He studied at the American Seminary for Contemporary Judaism and received rabbinic ordination in 2011 from Yeshiva Mesilat Yesharim.

Juan Marcos Bejarano Gutierrez was a board member of the Society for Crypto-Judaic Studies from 2011-2013. He is the author of *Secret Jews: The Complex Identity of Crypto-Jews and Crypto-Judaism*, *What is Kosher?* and *What is Jewish Prayer?* He is currently the director of the B'nai Anusim Center for Education at CryptoJudaism.com.

If you have enjoyed this book or others that are part of this series, please consider leaving a positive review on Amazon or Goodreads. A positive review helps spread the word and encourages others to study and learn something new.

Made in the USA
Columbia, SC
21 April 2020